carrousel confessions confusion

Roger Boltshauser

Otto Müller, Trudi Demut,
Hans Josephsohn

Studio Jan De Vylder
ETH Zürich D-ARCH

Koenig Books, London

Roger Boltshauser

Parallel Processes I

Right next to the edge of the block with our studio building on Dubsstrasse in Zurich, one can admire Ernst Gisel's studio house building on Wuhrstrasse. Like many turn-of-the-century buildings in our neighbourhood and our own studio building, it has brick facades. For many decades, it was the workplace and residence of artists Otto Müller and Trudi Demut, whose work can today be seen in the halls of the former freight depot of the Swiss Federal Railways in Zurich. A relief by Otto Müller still adorns the exterior facade of Gisel's studio house today.

I find the encounter with the works of Otto Müller and Trudi Demut a kind of coincidence. To this day, they are not only close to me geographically but continue to be a source of inspiration for me today. Especially the works created between the 1950s and 1980s are particularly important to me. The relatively flat, partly rather geometric wall reliefs that have been created by both artists during this period inspire me again and again for my own work and analyses. Some of the works of Müller and Demut seem to be coincidentally related to the original room casting models inspired by Luigi Moretti from the students of our design course at the University of Applied Sciences Chur and the Anhalt Dessau, which I later revised myself and cast in Tombak. During my time as a lecturer at the two schools, we dealt extensively with the topic of "space". We used castings of interiors to compare the properties of rooms from different origins and different eras. Our aim was to sharpen the perception of space as the basic experience of architecture, in order to create more specific spatial effects. Some of these studies were later documented by Aita Flury and myself in the publication "Elementares zum Raum / A Primer to Space" (2009).

Interestingly, from 1938 Otto Müller was also the teacher of Hans Josephsohn and later also of Trudi Demut, with whom he was in a relationship.. While the works of Hans Josephsohn have meanwhile become very well known and are represented by the internationally renowned Gallery Hauser and Wirth, those of Otto Müller and Trudi Demut have been forgotten. Surprisingly, the works produced during the 1950s by all three artists seem related. While the works of Hans Josephsohn—even the bas-reliefs of the 1950s—always had a figurative character, the works of Otto Müller and Trudi Demut—especially from the 1950s to 1970s—are more geometric and abstract, almost comparable to architectural models.

I am particularly interested in these works, as they have a highly plastic character: they impress with their massivity and materiality. They are often made of plaster and then painted over with paint. This is particularly interesting because they are intended as originals in this form and apparently should not serve as a template for a cast. This was different with Josephsohn: there are almost no coloured gypsum originals in the Sitterwerk in St. Gallen today. In the case of Otto Müller and Trudi Demut, a lack of money to cast these models was certainly one of the reasons for the missing casts. Opportunities for art in construction, which Otto Müller repeatedly received, for instance for Ernst Gisel, Albert Heinrich Steiner or Walter Maria Förderer, always came in handy. This work was then usually cast, lending the works the necessary robustness for their respective locations.

The works of Otto Müller—especially for the devotional space of the University of St. Gallen built between 1961 and 1966—which he was allowed to realise for the sculptor and architect Förderer, are for me the strongest creative phase. Müller produced a brass triptych in geometrical shapes as a bas-relief, as well as a sculpture in brass which mystically reconciles light and mass through its prismatic form. The reliefs and the objects created a dialogue with the geometry of the space and heighten it. The triptych appears in its luminous brass setting as a window into another room.

The cubic sculpture seems to find its continuation in the work "Three different figures on a pedestal", which he produced between 1962 and 1973 for the city of Zurich. Müller also created an axonometric drawing which illustrated the sculpture on two sides. Again, the work is reminiscent of concrete brutalist architectures, but in its formulation is simpler and more archaic, less intellectual, but rather shaped by a "primal sense" of massing and proportions. For Otto Müller it was always also a struggle to achieve the finished form. For example, after he won his first competition in 1940 for a bronze group of two workers, it took about 13 years until he could deliver these to the contractors. The work evolved in this time from a naturalistic version to a more abstract, more typifying style of design. From 1957, the first relief panels and full sculptures were then created, which presented geometric bodies or incorporated elementary geometrical signs in relief. Müller was fascinated by the archaic and pre-classical sculptures of what he deemed as the "happy" Greeks. He was looking for effortless virtuosity, not “forced” intellectualism as he said.

Presumably it was also what interested Otto Müller in the work of

Trudi Demut, who had begun working as an autodidact with him in the studio. What was for Otto Müller a lifelong struggle for simplicity and lightheartedness, for Demut seemed effortless. Otto Müller was already amazed by her first work, a half-figure made of stone, which she completed in 1949 in his studio. Demut also created bas-reliefs starting in 1956, as well as geometric sculptures, later also large-scale drawings.

Even today, the works of Trudi Demut appear even more direct than those of Otto Müller. In the shadow of well-known artist friends such as Otto Müller, Hans Aeschbacher and Leo Oesterle, she created an oeuvre that was overshadowed by them for a long time. Even in the 1990 issue of the magazine "Du" about Otto Müller, Trudi Demut was hardly mentioned.

In Fritz Billeter's publication (1988) on Demut, for example, the following encounter is noted: when the art historian Adolf Max Vogt returned from the US and was first faced with the work of Demut, he was apparently so impressed that he was convinced of seeing the first examples of European Minimal Art. But the affinity is only superficial, as well as the apparent similarity to constructive concrete art. Demut always modelled the plaster by hand: the objects were shaped and "given a soul" in this sense. Demut is said to have titled her designs as "Torsi", which brings the work into the figurative. On her travels with Otto Müller, she had seen the ancient temple ruins of Paestum and Selinunte. These were an inspiration for her sculpture "Olympic Still Life" from 1987, placed in a Zurich sports complex. Part of this work is reminiscent of a Greek column, fragmented over four elements. This piece discusses the archetypes of architecture that Demut powerfully knew how to translate. Already the pieces "Relief I" and "Relief II" (both 1959) are reminiscent of columns, as well as other sculptures, such as "Plastik I" (1969) with a cross motif in bronze. Further reliefs such as the "Tafel I" (1961), made of English cement and the "Tafel II" (1962), made of coloured gypsum, are reminiscent of torsos or column shafts, which in turn testifies to their affinity with architecture.

Both Otto Müller and Trudi Demut were engaged in a perpetual search that allowed them to process and interpret the same motifs again and again - always knowing that they would never arrive completely. Paul Nizon described in the preface to Müller's 1980 publication that their oeuvre hardly changed over long periods. Minimal additions and removals, increases and tightening ... Creating spontaneously, bringing only the first sketch to fruition. It is a way of working that was also particular to Hans Josephsohn, who also worked on the same motifs for a long time.

Starting in 2006, I started plastering over the Moretti-inspired cast models from the students with gypsum and further working on them. Starting from the polystyrene works, new reliefs emerged, based on the original analysis, but formulated in an abstract and sculptural way. In the meantime, I had met Hans Josephsohn personally and acquired three smaller works from him. Josephsohn invited me to the Sitterwerk in St. Gallen to hand over a completed small half-figure that had not yet been cast when I had bought it. After handing over the piece and giving me a tour of his showroom, he also explained the current possibilities of casting techniques. It quickly became clear to me that it would be possible to cast the relatively fragile, plaster-covered polystyrene reliefs here through a special casting process. In 2010, I decided to cast the first two models—'learning from Como'—for the architecture exhibition during the dOCUMENTA (13) in Kassel in 2012. These were my first works, which were cast in the Sitterwerk in Tombak and then shown in Kassel. The light, gypsum polystyrene reliefs had finally found a form that I felt did justice to their strong and sculptural quality, whilst dealing with the actual lack of mass and materiality.

In 2012, additional works were added, which were shown in the Architekturgalerie in Berlin. By 2015, around 12 relief works had been created, which essentially refer to concrete buildings. In addition to the referential reliefs, which refer to Giuseppe Terragni, Auguste Perret or Gunnar Asplund, reliefs have also been created based on our own work - in particular the residential tower in Hirzenbach. The reliefs were also part of own design process. Series of reliefs such as those of Auguste Perret, on the other hand, served as a direct inspiration for the façade design of the skyscrapers on the Europaallee in Zurich due to their strongly abstract interpretation. In 2015, I created the first free reliefs, which I continue to work on until today. It was exciting for me to find out that if I broke away from real references with my relief work, these freer works could then become the inspiration for subsequent architectural designs. Here, too, one can speak of a perpetual process in which the work is constantly being developed and reinterpreted.

Roger Boltshauser

Otto Müller, Trudi Demut, Hans Josephsohn

Filip Dujardin

August 22, 2018

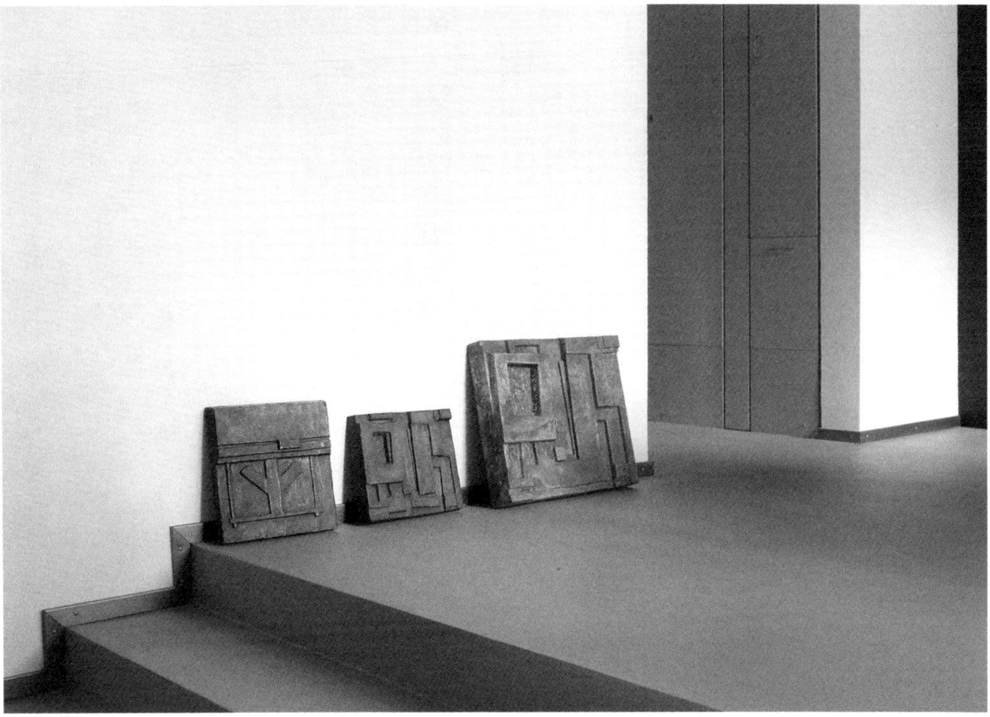

Inge Vinck

Relief for Otto. For Roger

Roger Boltshauser

Parallel Processes II

Otto Müller

Relief I, 1954
Gips. Höhe 171,5 cm, Breite 123 cm, Tiefe 9 cm
40
Relief II, 1955
Gips bemalt. Höhe 190 cm, Breite 140 cm, Tiefe 9 cm
41

Relief II, 1957
Bronze, Höhe 120 cm, Breite 85 cm, Tiefe 7 cm

Relief I, 1960
Messing, Höhe 91 cm, Breite 47 cm, Tiefe 6 cm

Relief II, 1957–1965
Messing, Höhe 209 cm, Breite 1907 cm, Tiefe 9,5 cm

Relief II, 1960
Messing, Höhe 73 cm, Breite 77, Tiefe 11 cm

Begehbare Betonplastik im Freibad Auhof, 1957–1959
Sichtbeton, Höhe 180 cm, Breite 950 cm, Tiefe 800 cm

Plastik I, 1965
Messing, Höhe 59 cm, Breite 14 cm, Tiefe 18 cm

Plastik I, 1963
Messing, Höhe 47 cm, Breite 18 cm, Tiefe 25 cm

Relief II, 1966
Bronze, Höhe 100 cm, Breite 93 cm, Tiefe 6,5 cm

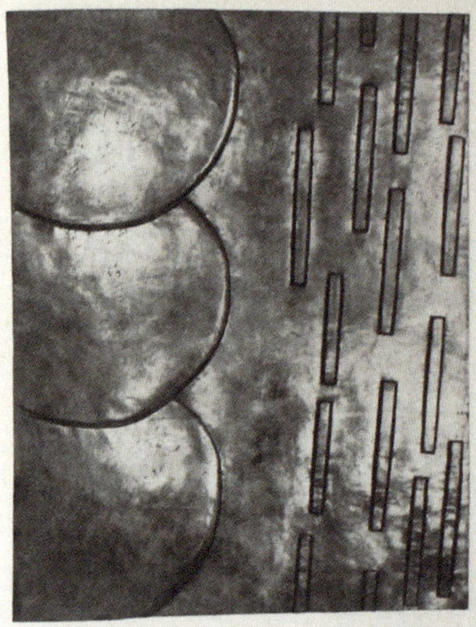

Grosse Messingtafel, 1972
Messing, Höhe 260 cm, Breite 210 cm, Tiefe 10 cm

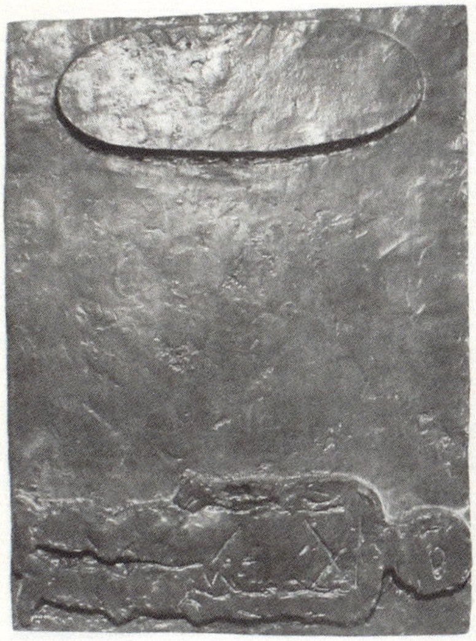

Relief «Kleiner Toter», 1962
Blei, Höhe 78 cm, Breite 61 cm, Tiefe 6 cm

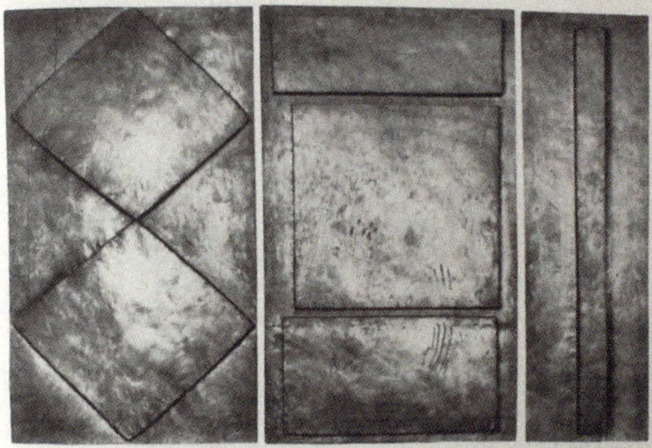

«Triptychon», 1962
Messing, Höhe 165 cm, Breite 265 cm, Tiefe 9 cm

Otto Müller

Ich bin im August 1905 im Zeichen des Löwen geboren. Ich liebe den Sommer. Ich habe den grössten Teil meines Lebens in Zürich verbracht. Seit meinem 17. Altersjahr beschäftigt mich die Bildhauerei mit allen Konsequenzen. Ich hoffe, ich könne es noch recht lange so halten, es bleibe mir noch viel Zeit, ich habe noch viel zu tun.

1978

Biographische Notizen

1905	in Thalwil geboren
1921-25	Bildhauerlehre in Zürich
1926	erste Reise nach Florenz
1929	arbeitet zusammen mit seinem Bruder Heinrich Müller in einem Atelier in Thalwil. Zugleich ist er bis 1937 als Kinoreklamemaler in Zürich tätig
1931-33	Mitarbeiter im Atelier von Karl Geiser
1931-38	alljährliche Studienreisen nach Paris
1933	Bezug des ersten eigenen Ateliers in Zürich
1937-38	arbeitet für die Aussenrenovation der Kathedrale in St. Gallen
1940	1. Preis im Wettbewerb für eine Freiplastik vor dem kantonalen Technikum in Winterthur und Auftrag für eine Bronzegruppe «Zwei Arbeiter»
1944	Conrad-Ferdinand-Meyer-Preis, in der Folge entstehen aus Wettbewerben verschiedene Plastiken
1953	sind die Arbeiten «Winterthurer Gruppe», «Kuh mit Kälblein» und «Hirsch» abgeschlossen
1961-66	räumliche und künstlerische Gestaltung des paritätischen Andachtsraumes in der neuen Hochschule St. Gallen für Wirtschafts- und Sozialwissenschaften
1964	Premio del Fiorino der Unione Fiorentina, Florenz
1970	mit Hans Fischli zusammen, räumliche und künstlerische Gestaltung des Eingangshofes im Stadtspital Triemli, Zürich
1970-72	entsteht die grosse Messingtafel für die Eingangshalle der neuen Kantonalbank an der Bahnhofstrasse in Zürich
1973-74	entstehen zwei Messingplastiken in einem Betonrahmen im neuen Primarschulhaus Eschenbach SG
1977-80	architektonische und künstlerische Gestaltung eines Platzes in der Grünau, Zürich
1978-79	Platzgestaltung mit Bronzeplastik «Kopf im Gehäuse» vor dem neuen Völkerkundemuseum der Universität, Zürich
seit 1947	immer wieder Reisen nach Italien

DIE ZEITSCHRIFT DER KULTUR
du
Heft Nr. 1
Januar 1990
Meier
und
Müller

Ich stelle ein Bild vom
Menschen hin.
Ein Bild vom Menschen,
gross und schön
und aus Bronze, die hält.
Ein Bild vom intakten
Menschen, dass wir in ihm uns
wieder erkennen,
und uns erinnern an das
Verlorene,
und wieder einsehen
und wissen,
dass der Mensch uns das
Nächste ist.

Wir haben es seit langem
vergessen,
sind abgedriftet auf falsche
Spuren,
ins Chaos getrieben durch
hybrides Tun,
weit weg von allem
Menschlichen.
Unser Tun ist die totale
Bedrohung,
wir sind bestimmt von
Sachzwängen,
völlig beherrscht von der
Maschine,
das Geld versklavt uns und
raubt uns die Freiheit,
die Ausbeutung schafft Unruhe
und Empörung,
die Folter ist zutiefst böse,
der Krieg schrecklich und
unmenschlich,
Liebe und Vernunft wie
nie gewesen.

Darum dies vergessene Bild
des zeitlos Gültigen
und der menschlichen Würde.
Otto Müller, 1985

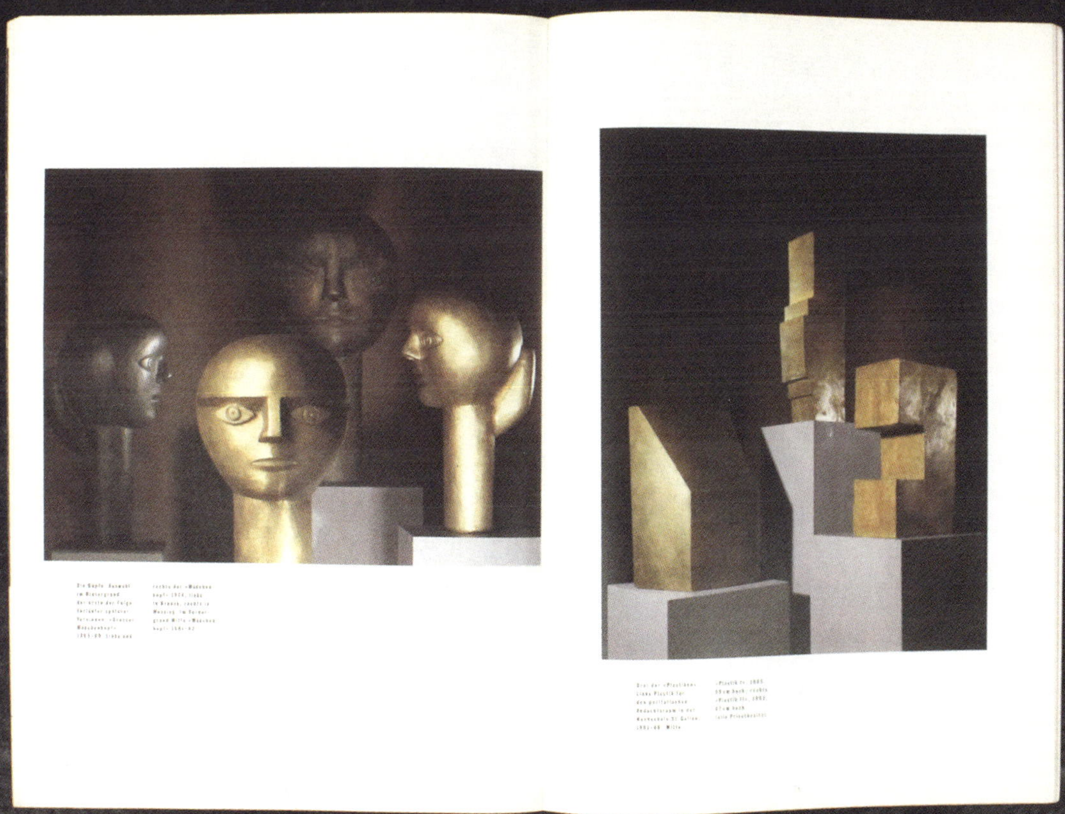

ihr selber her ausdeutbar» Reduktion der Welt, respektive dessen, was über sie ausgesagt wird, auf wenige wesentliche Elemente, auf das Mindest-zu-Sagende; trotzdem ist diese Welt vollständig.

In ihr wartet bereits – im Gegensatz zu den frühen Bildnissen – ein Ansatz zu Widerspruch, Aufbegehren. Schon das Kälbchen oder Kühlein reckt den Kopf trotzig oder anklagend nach oben; ausdrücklicher formuliert wird dieser Ansatz im nächsten Schritt, in den Reliefs der mittleren sechziger Jahre; in den Reliefs der «Stillen Toten», der «Drei Toten», der «Bedrohung». Otto Müller reagiert hier, spät aber eindringlich, auf den nun schon zwanzig Jahre zurückliegenden Weltkrieg, auf seiten der Opfer, ohne die Mörder explizit anzuklagen. Jene, die längst begraben sind, werden es auf Müllers Tafeln noch einmal, werden noch einmal gebettet, nicht in Ruhe, nicht in Frieden; sie werden unbequem hingelagert, manchmal geschichtet, sogar zu Haufen; andere haben unendlichen Raum über sich – oder Grabgewicht, Zeit und Geschichte, die sie niederdrückt. Müller ist schon sechzigjährig – und bewältigt jetzt, vielleicht im Zusammenhang mit seiner Psychoanalyse, die damals seit einigen Jahren abgeschlossen war, das Trauma seines Jahrhunderts. In diesem Augenblick ist Otto Müller ein bedeutender Bildhauer geworden.

In kubischen Gestaltungen, «Chlötzli» sagt er ihnen und nennt sie offiziell «Plastik» oder «Figur», geht Müller, parallel zur Arbeit an den «Toten»-Tafeln, weiter den Weg, den er mit der Reduktion der Kühlein-Reliefs eingeschlagen hatte. Diesmal in der vollen Form. Was ihn hier interessiert, sind Volumen, Form, Oberfläche – aber vor allem wiederum die Vereinfachung auf das nur noch lakonisch Sagbare, das Wort anstelle des Satzes. Am deutlichsten und schönsten in einem radikal einfachen Körper, den er für den paritätischen Andachtsraum in der St. Galler Hochschule macht (1961/66). Dieser Körper schliesst seine Botschaft wie ein grosses Rätsel in sich ein, kommuniziert mit dem Betrachter freilich durch eine atmende Haut – und erinnert in seinem lakonischen Da-Sein an jenen rätselvollen Klotz in Stanley Kubricks Film «Odyssee im Weltraum», in welchem auch eine Art Summe des Weltgeheimnisses eingeschlossen ist.

Im Nachhinein sehen ganze Werkgruppen von Otto Müller wie Warmlaufen, wie Vorbereitung auf das Schwierigste aus. Das Bedeutendste, das Geglückteste kommt erst ganz am Ende dieses langen, mit gemessenem Schritt gegangenen Weges. 1969 nämlich wird der erste der Köpfe, mit denen sich Otto Müller in den folgenden zwanzig Jahren beschäftigen wird, fertig. Wiederum hat Müller sechs Jahre lang – hier ist es für einmal keine Floskel – mit der Form gerungen. Nun steht sie da, bereit dazu, variiert und weiterentwickelt zu werden bis zu den Höhepunkten – dem «Kopf im Gehäuse» im alten Zürcher Botanischen Garten

Plakat fürs Kino Orient (oben links). Oben rechts mit Leo Besterle an der Arbeit für die Steinplastik

«Nub mit Nüßlein». Seine Arbeit am «Stehenden Mädchen», in der Steinfassung zerstört

(1978–79), dem «Mädchenkopf» (1981–82) und dem kolossalen, über drei Meter hohen Kopf im Hof des Rathauses von Fellbach bei Stuttgart.

Das Monumentale ist erreicht. Wie die gewaltigen, unerklärbaren Köpfe der Osterinsel stehen diese Häupter dem Betrachter entgegen, wuchtig, frontal, unerschütterlich, Abbilder des Menschen schlechthin, auch wenn sie merkwürdig versteckt unter ihrer Tarnung als «Mädchenköpfe» Züge ihres Schöpfers tragen.

Noch einmal, während auf der vielbeachteten Kunstszene andere Temperamente sich zu tummeln beginnen, während alles geht, was jung, neu, wild, bewegt, verwegen ist, Masche hier, Masche dort, ist da ein knorriger Charakter am Werk, versucht einer, gegen die Moden des müden, eklektischen Ästhetizismus seiner Bronze einen gültigen, allgemeinen Ausdruck abzutrotzen. hat dieser Otto Müller, vergraben in Zürichs Unauffälligkeit, so etwas wie Condition humaine im Sinn, riskiert er so etwas Altmodisches wie das Abbild des Menschen. Freilich kein realistisches mehr.

Herausgerissen aus der Materie blicken diese Gesichter dem Jahrhundert furchtlos und standfest entgegen. In ihrem bohrenden Blick eine vieldeutige

Im Felde ... Rechts Arbeit am «Relief 5», 1957. Bild links: Auf dem Werkplatz zusammen mit Weggefährtin Trudi Demel

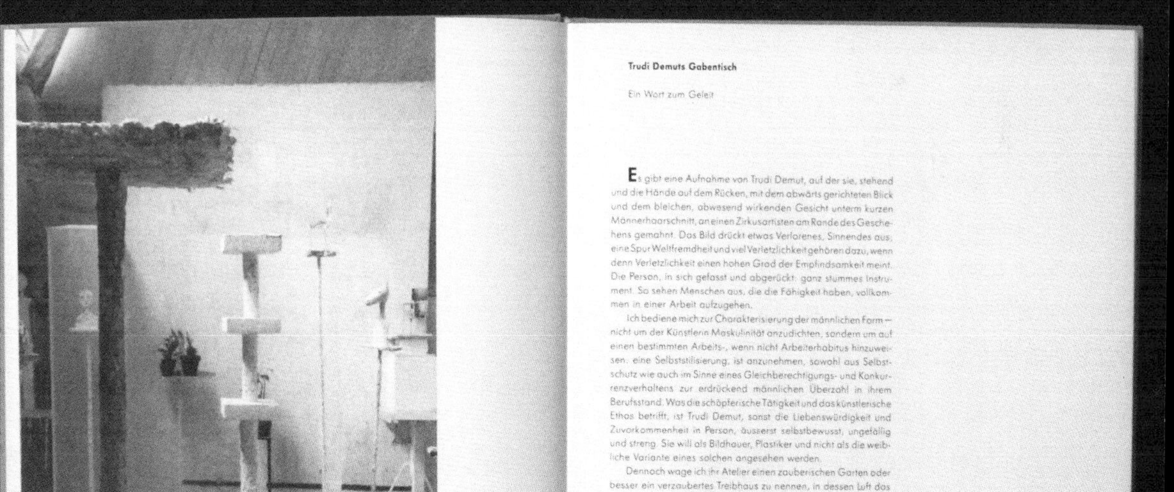

Trudi Demuts Gabentisch

Ein Wort zum Geleit

Es gibt eine Aufnahme von Trudi Demut, auf der sie, stehend und die Hände auf dem Rücken, mit dem abwärts gerichteten Blick und dem bleichen, abwesend wirkenden Gesicht unterm kurzen Männerhaarschnitt, an einen Zirkusartisten am Rande des Geschehens gemahnt. Das Bild drückt etwas Verlorenes, Sinnendes aus; eine Spur Weltfremdheit und viel Verletzlichkeit gehören dazu, wenn denn Verletzlichkeit einen hohen Grad der Empfindsamkeit meint. Die Person, in sich gefasst und abgerückt: ganz stummes Instrument. So sehen Menschen aus, die die Fähigkeit haben, vollkommen in einer Arbeit aufzugehen.

Ich bediene mich zur Charakterisierung der männlichen Form – nicht um der Künstlerin Maskulinität anzudichten, sondern um auf einen bestimmten Arbeits-, wenn nicht Arbeiterhabitus hinzuweisen: eine Selbststilisierung, ist anzunehmen, sowohl aus Selbstschutz wie auch im Sinne eines Gleichberechtigungs- und Konkurrenzverhaltens zur erdrückend männlichen Überzahl in ihrem Berufsstand. Was die schöpferische Tätigkeit und das künstlerische Ethos betrifft, ist Trudi Demut, sonst die Liebenswürdigkeit und Zuvorkommenheit in Person, äusserst selbstbewusst, ungefällig und streng. Sie will als Bildhauer, Plastiker und nicht als die weibliche Variante eines solchen angesehen werden.

Dennoch wage ich ihr Atelier einen zauberischen Garten oder besser ein verzaubertes Treibhaus zu nennen, in dessen Luft das weibliche Element unverkennbar ist; schwer zu sagen, ob es an der heiteren Reinlichkeit liegt, der Abwesenheit von Gewalt, der Aura einer hegerischen Liebe, die die Wesen gedeihen, atmen und wachsen lässt. Die Wesen sind spinnenbeinige Tische und gehörnte Tierköpfe, und das vielverzweigte Geweih und die sondenförmigen Beine setzen sich um in den Eindruck spriessenden, knospenden Lebens, eines gefühligen Luftwurzelwerks, vor allem in der gemilderten Helle, einem Licht, das das Reinste ausstrahlt. Darum das Bild vom Gewächshaus.

7

Plastik I, Gips, [illegible] cm hoch, 1964–1965

Plastik I, Sockel mit Aufsicht, photographische Variante

Plastik I, Bronze, 79 cm hoch, 1969

Bronze-Plastik, Bronze, 65 cm hoch, 1965–1973

Relief I, Messing, 128 × 69 cm, 1958

Relief II, Bronze (Abbildung Gipsmodell), 123 × 65 cm, 1958

Kaltnadel-Radierung, 20 × 17,5 cm, 1962

Kaltnadel-Radierung, 10 × 10,5 cm, 1964

Tafel II, Gips, 125 × 102 cm, 1961–1967

Tafel I, Bronze, 156 × 135 cm, 1971, Maternité, Triemli-Spital

melsband, an das auf der Horizontlinie die Erde stösst, umbrafarbig, mit Grau- und Blautönen durchsetzt. Das Himmelsband erscheint leichtgewichtig, die Erdzone materiell-schwer, als Struktur von Pinselflecken und -striemen. Diese Landschaft drückt (noch) nicht Sehnsucht aus, wohl aber Ferne und Weite, unsentimental, gewissermassen als objektiv-räumlichen Tatbestand. Die Farben des Bildes sind für Trudi Demuts Malerei überhaupt bezeichnend. Sie liebt Grau, Weiss, Blaunuancen und Erdtöne. Nie bricht sie in Überschwang aus, ein helles Türkis, ein Lachsrot, ein Rosa oder Violettrosa ist schon das höchste.

Trudi Demut bevorzugt die grosse singuläre Einzelform, der sich wenige, kleinere Formen zuordnen: die Insel als oval hochragender Bergrücken auf einem das Meer andeutenden Sockel oder Band, die schroffe, einsame Felsspitze, von schmalen, spindelförmigen Wolken umzogen oder auch ohne Wolken ins Leere stossend. «Mir schweben Bilder vor, die hell und leicht, aber tief ernst sind: Weltfarben, Welternst», lautet eine Tagebucheintragung.

Die Landschaften von Trudi Demut meinen etwas Diesseitiges, das aber umfassend. Sie lassen sich geographisch nicht näher bestimmen, dürften jedoch eher im kühlen Norden als unter einer glücklichen Mittelmeersonne liegen. Die Künstlerin selbst hat sich dahin geäussert, dass ihr zuweilen leere und karge schottische Gegenden (die sie auf Reisen kennen und lieben lernte) vor Augen gestanden seien, aber auch die von konventionellen Landschaftsstaffagen befreiten Bilder eines Caspar David Friedrich. Sie aber, «ein Gemisch von Ratio und Romantik», wolle die ihren noch «kristalliner».

Aus Trudi Demuts Berg- und Inselbilder mögen einem Vereinsamung, aber auch das stoische Lebensgefühl des Durchhaltens entgegentreten. Gleichzeitig symbolisieren solche Landschaften Orte der Entrückung und der inneren Sammlung, wo Zerstreuung und Trivialität des Alltags die Künstlerin nicht mehr erreichen. Es sind Orte, wo sie ihren Ursprung, Goethe würde sagen ihre Naivetät, wiederfindet.

Fritz Billeter

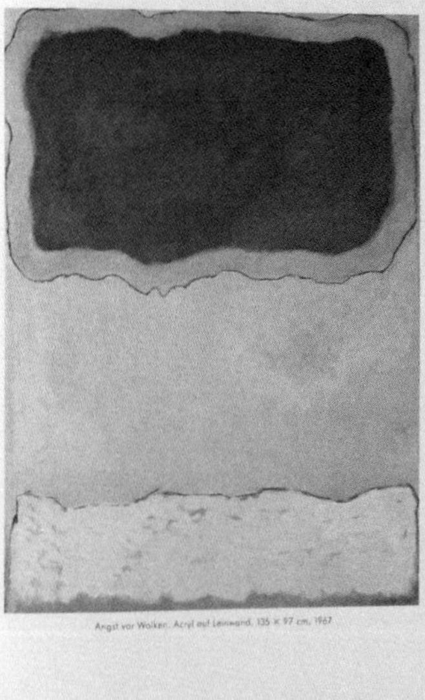

Angst vor Wolken, Acryl auf Leinwand, 135 × 97 cm, 1967

[illegible]

Atelier mit Sicht auf den Hof, Sommer 1985

Trudi Demut, 1981

Biographische Notizen

1927	in Zürich geboren und aufgewachsen Besuch der Primar- und Sekundarschule
1943 – 1945	kaufmännische Lehre
1945 – 1946	kaufmännische Angestellte
1947 – 1948	in England bei Kindern und Besuch einer Bildhauer-Abendklasse an der Kunstgewerbeschule von Kingston on Thames
1948	zurück in Zürich Volontärin bei einem Steinbildhauer. Auf dessen Werkplatz Begegnung mit den Bildhauern Otto Müller und Hans Aeschbacher. Daneben, um finanziell unabhängig zu sein, während 17 Jahren Halbtagsstelle auf einem Büro
1948 – 1952	Schülerin von Otto Müller, ab
1953	eigenes Atelier im Atelier-Haus an der Wuhrstrasse in Zürich

Kesselhaus
Josephsohn
Herausgeber/Editors
Udo Kittelmann
Felix Lehner

120

121

138

139

painting, I also see it, but it isn't any feat – finding Fouquet's Madonna in Gent or a Titian magnificent, we don't have to argue about that. But with some young artist it's really difficult. And I am convinced that many art house directors can't see it either with total clarity. I don't want to pass judgment on anyone for that, because I know how difficult it is myself.

With the widespread ›anything goes‹, which means that everything is possible, the criteria naturally become more relaxed. Can you name some contemporary sculpture about which you could say that it stands out as interesting?

Yes that, you know, I don't know. When people are young, until 40 perhaps, then they have the need to see what is being made. Today I don't know most of them at all.

Amine Haase conducted this conversation with Hans Josephsohn on 20 May 2005 in Cologne, where the Diözesanmuseum organized a celebration for the 85th birthday of the Swiss sculptor.

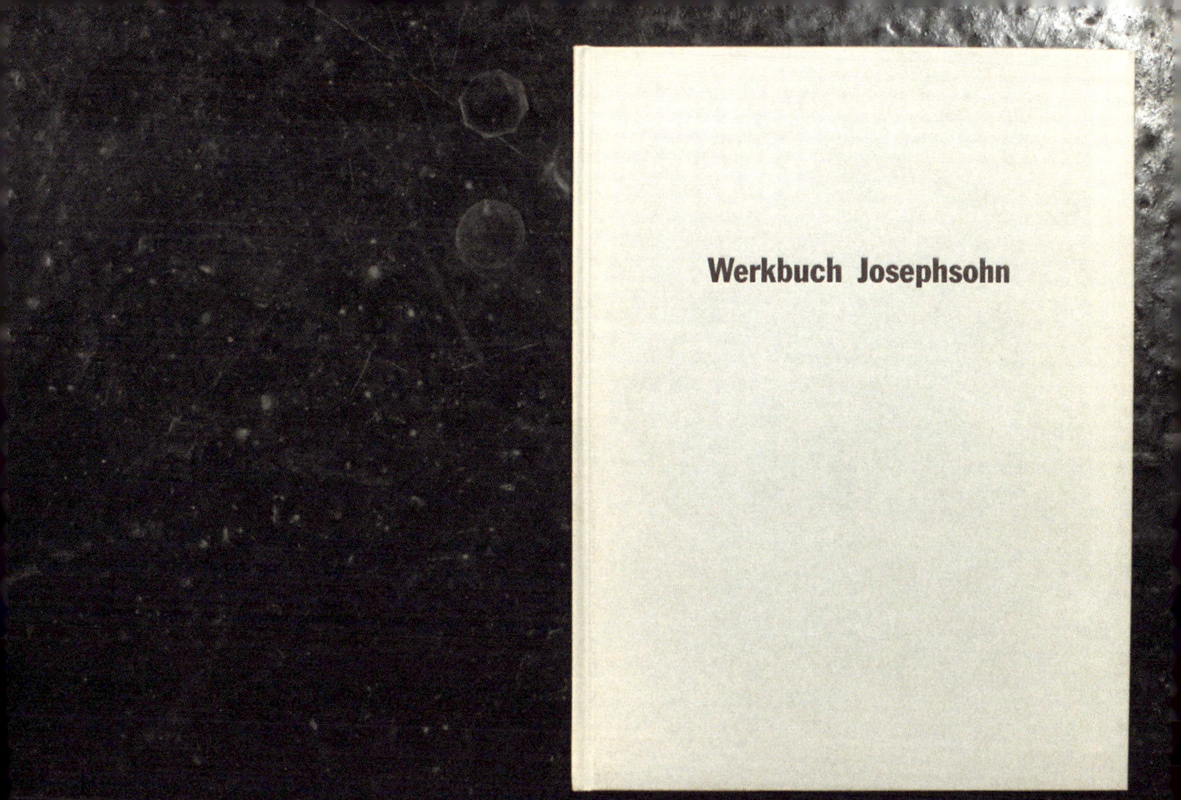
Werkbuch Josephsohn

Kolumba, 13. Mai bis 21. August 2005

Martin Tschanz

The Relief between Art and Architecture. Walter Maria Förderer Otto Müller Roger Boltshauser

In around 1960, the art of Otto Müller provided an artistic medium with which to compensate for the loss of the architectural relief. Today, it serves as the key to rediscovering the spatial design possibilities in architectural structures.

In 1964 the book "Kirchenbau—von heute—für morgen?" [Church Buildings: From Today - For Tomorrow?] was published, it had been written by Walter Maria Förderer[1], one of the most successful church architects of his time. However, the cover is not graced by a church, but rather a non-representational relief. In the upright format plate by the sculptor Otto Müller, one sees an irregular rectangular form and an upwards-facing semi-circle. Both forms seem rather imprecise. They relate to each other, touch the outer edges and gravity also seems to play a role.

With the subtitle "Fragen heutiger Architektur und Kunst" [Questions in Contemporary Architecture and Art], Förderer hints at the significance of this seemingly surprising cover image. Convinced that the church has lost its dominant role in society, he pleads for more modesty. The church should move closer to the people rather than try to compensate for the loss of its own language. With this in mind, he proposed building churches within housing estates, embedding them within the anonymous structure of the blocks and towers. Such "house churches" do not have "to be like heaven in the first place", but rooms of a special kind "that seek to create a community"[2].

The means with which to distinguish these rooms within the structure of standardised architecture should if nothing else be provided by the fine arts, whereby "craftsmanship and artistic intelligence, as well as sensitivity"[3] would supplement this. Through a string of fictive, roughly-sketched examples Förderer showed how "artistic means"[4] could be used in the service of architecture. He did not believe in explicitly Christian art, but was instead convinced that works without "specific symbolic meaning could represent religious artwork to us today". Whilst symbolic art was downgraded to simple decoration, all "art created from real feeling and experience [w]as deeply religious"[5]. As an example and also proof of this, was, amongst others, the non-

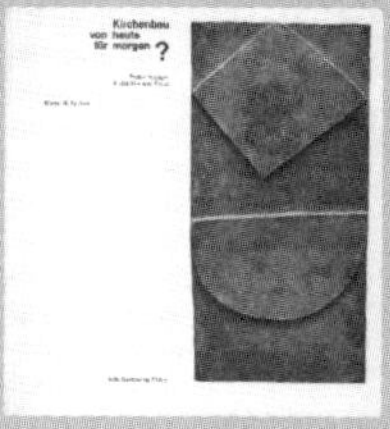

1. Förderer, Walter M., *Kirchenbau von heute für morgen? Fragen heutiger Architektur und Kunst*, Zürich 1964.
Cover with "Relief I" (1960) by Otto Müller.

2. ibidem, p. 60.

3. ibidem.

4. ibidem, p. 80.

5. ibidem, p. 110.

representational relief by Otto Müller.

The Prayer Room in the University of St. Gallen

Förderer was able to build upon his own experiences with these basic reflections. In the campus of the University of St. Gallen, built like a small town, it is not the ecclesiastical spaces that form the spatial and symbolic centre, but the library and the meeting room of the stairwell. Although there is a non-denominational prayer room, this is not located in a central location, but in the base area, adjacent to administrative rooms[6]. All the same, it divides its entrance loggia with the auditorium, so that its position is ambivalent: on the one hand, it lies underground, embedded within the standardised structure of the school, on the other hand, it forms a kind of crypt in relation to the prestigious hall.

The architects Förderer, Otto and Zwimpfer placed the design of this room in the hands of the artist Otto Müller. He arranged three independent works from 1962, which came from three different work groups[7]. The theme of the relief is formative, not only because two of the works belong to this genre. The third, "Plastik 1" in gilded brass, stands under the square stairwell. A mighty pedestal creates a space for this work under the stairs. As a result, the object, which in itself is fully plastic, is integrated into a relief design, just as the sculptor and theoretician Adolf Hildebrand, whose writings had been extensively studied by Müller, had called for in "The Problem of Form in the Fine Arts"[8]. The skewed view of the underside of the staircase influences the perception of the golden, shimmering body and vice versa, analogous to the two fields, which are incorporated into the concrete sculpture. Despite the corporality of "Plastik I", it is not possible to clearly decide where the architecture begins and where the artistic intervention ends.

The same applies to the cuboid and the concrete wall console, which could serve as a prayer bench with their leather upholstery. A simple line, notched from the console into the trowelled wall surface, frames the praying man's head or an object placed there, linking the bench, the room, and the actions performed here. Lastly, the outward appearance of the prayer room is also shaped by a relief design. It incorporates the single, narrow window into a larger façade with blind windows, so that it fits into the regular grid of the architecture without blending into or merging with it.

Art Instead of Architecture

Otto Müller's interest in the relief was shared by Förderer. In the entrance area of the prayer room and auditorium, the façade columns free themselves from their constructive function and combine with the layered concrete to form a playful composition. In later buildings, the relief becomes an integral and defining element of the architecture. It is particularly impressive in the church of St. Nicolas

6. *Die Handelshochschule St. Gallen*, in: *Das Werk* 1953, Issue 8, p. 297-315; «Neue Kunstwerke in der Handelshochschule St. Gallen», in: *Das Werk*, 1966, Issue 10, p. 209-412.

7. Billeter, Fritz, *Der Plastiker Otto Müller, ein Überlebender in dieser Zeit*, Zürich 1983.

8. Hildebrand, Adolf, *Das Problem der Form in der bildenden Kunst*, Strassburg 1893.

Otto Müller: *Non-denominational prayer room*, University of St. Gallen (architects: Förderer, Otto and Zwimpfer, 1961-1966).

in Hérémence. The mighty wall behind the altar is multi-layered, starting from the square block, in which the eternal light is incorporated, to the deep niche holding a historical cross. The relief not only integrates different elements such as organs, seats or figurines of Saints into the architecture, it also mediates between the parts of the wall, directs the view (and thus the perception), animates the surface and creates a play of light and shadow. Last but not least, it brings the small-scale haptic experiences with the large-scale spatial whole into a perceptible relationship.

One may think of Alberti's remark in this multi-layered design, that sometimes "one wall serves to support the other, like the fur, to the garment"[9]. This reference should not be surprising. Of course, the relief has always played a central role in architecture, even in the classical architectural tradition. It is not by chance that designing the profiles has always been one of the most important and highly valued tasks for an architect. The old treatises are full of references as to how profiling can govern the relationship of different parts to each other and how they can determine the character of a building.

For Förderer, however, the language of the supporting or crowning cornice, the pilasters and the egg-and-dart moulding was no longer accessible. He considered insurmountable the break modernity had made with tradition. Therefore, he had to solve the problems that had once been solved by the classical formal vocabulary and the traditional ornamentation with his own, new means. He relied on his personal sensitivity as a sculptor and treated the building as a large sculpture, which he designed according to his own perception and sensibility. He trusted that the work would become valid due to his own specific contemporaneity and humanity as an artist.

The means he used are elementary: hollow and solid, light and dark, line and surface, right angles and their halving. The building became an enlarged cast of the model developed in the studio. This leads to an immediacy of the expression akin to the use of the archaic in works by Otto Müller, even if an equal calmness and simplicity were not achieved, and probably not strived for at all.

Förderer felt that building in his time was deeply divided. On the one hand, he saw the path of rationalisation and standards, culminating in industrialised construction. On the other hand, he saw architecture as art, which frees itself as far as possible from the conditions of purpose and economy, and is based entirely on the personal sensitivity of its creator. Ideally, such a "high purposelessness" could emerge "that could really be a symbol of today's general human vision"[10].

The problem of combining this with practical purposes, especially those of ecclesiastical liturgy, was countered by Förderer with as few stipulations as possible in favour of the function. So, in Hérémence, he replaced the concrete sacral landscape—consisting of the altar, lectern and podium—with a wooden installation, shortly before its execution. However, one cannot fail to link his works to his own statement that "hypertrophy of architectural form

9. Alberti, Leon Battista, *On the art of Building in Ten Books*, Cambridge Mass. 1988, (Book VI, Chapter 12).

10. ibidem, p. 52.

Walter M. Förderer: St. Nicolas church, Hérémence 1962-1971.

does not add to the expressiveness of church construction"[11]. In fact, he understood them less as churches or schools, and more as works of the artist Walter Maria Förderer[12].

Towards a New Synthesis

The gap between standardised, purposeful building and the architecture of a "necessary purposelessness" was considered by Förderer to be unbridgeable: for him, there was the convention established in the design of mass production, and free art. The problematic nature of this perspective and its consequences has indeed made itself clear in the 'star architecture' of recent years[13].

In the course of its history, however, architecture has found its identity again and again precisely through not only fulfilling purposes but also exploring "necessary purposelessness". Just think of the classical column, whose nature is certainly not only the practical and symbolic realisation of its load-bearing functions. It has always been regarded also as analogous to the human body, a representation of cosmic harmony and independent sculpture.

At this point, it seems to me, the reliefs by Roger Boltshauser begin by hinting at the realm of "necessary purposelessness" in architecture. Inspired by the reliefs of Otto Müller, architectural structures we are accustomed to reading as tectonic systems are transformed into a compact, homogeneous casting. As a result, the variety and diversity of the components fade into the background, ignoring the hierarchies and functional contexts on which the rationalist view of modern architecture had concentrated. What remains is the spatial effect of the relief: the composition of the protruding and recessed lines and surfaces, which guide the perception and affect the observer.

This view on architecture is no less reductive than that of functionalism. It also focuses on a partial aspect of the complex whole. As a corrective, however, this seems useful at the present time, perhaps even necessary. The artistic perspective helps to rediscover the intrinsic value and the inherent laws of the creative-spatial qualities in traditional architecture, which has long been blinded by an unfortunate tendency towards simplification. It opens up a path of renewal, which in turn leads to an archaism, but this time it is based not on expediency and construction, but on spatial design through relief. Through a small detour into the world of art, one can gain the freedom to reinterpret the instruments of architecture that are rooted in a tradition that integrates many sources, to achieve those spatial qualities that Förderer had to achieve through personal means. This opens up the perspective of a renewed form of architecture as spatial design, which as a synthesis closes the supposed gap between building and art. The architecture of Roger Boltshauser provides us with good examples of this notion.

11. ibidem, p. 39.

12. Bächer, Max, *Walter M. Förderer, Architektur - Skulptur*, Neuchâtel 1975, p. 29, 117, 139.

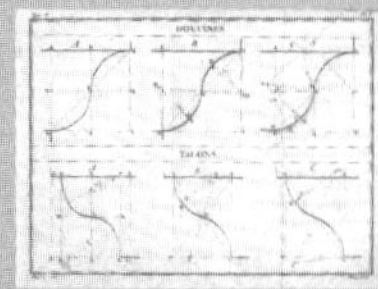

Jacques-François Blondel: Cours d'architecture, Paris 1771-1777, Bd. 1, Tav. V. (ETH-Bibliothek Zürich, e-rara.ch)

13. At the end of the twentieth century Jacques Herzog, much like Förderer, considered a split between star architecture and generic building: «Mit allen Sinnen spüren – Jacques Herzog in conversation with Sabine Kraft and Christian Kühn», in: Arch+ 7.1998, p. 32-39.

Roger Boltshauser: Krämeracker school, Uster, 2018.

carrousel
confessions
confusion

Carrousel

Carrousel was first an exhibition at ETH advvt held in 2015. The exhibition was divided in three parts. One was about seven interventions in the space of the gta. One was about showing the work of almost forty Belgian architects we liked; revealing through this selection ourselves, our interests, our attitude. One was about showing our own work; we decided to show in the cabinet, behind the wooden wall. Carrousel setting ran for one year, hosting other exhibitions by gta. Each the same yet different. Every exhibition leaving a trace.

Carrousel is now the furniture of our office at ETH, since we arrived in summer 2017. We cut the wall in pieces and we arranged tables, bookshelves, archive, paravents. Together with some of the furnitures of the following exhibitions that took place in the setting we made for the gta. Office kgdvs' bistro chairs, Shinohara's white tables, Dan Graham's sofa. Working with the existing things, catching traces, collecting objects.

Carrousel is going to be a series of books. Again revealing both our colleagues' personal interests and our own.

In the form of confessions.

Confessions

Confessing is something personal.

Confessions are about
something embarrassing or confusing
love, at least for a moment
something abandoned or refurbished
something which is not a sign of the times
something badly published or not at all
something not easy to clean
something we do not know much about

and if you do not find anything that matches any of these rules
you can choose one of your works
that is embarrassing
or
that matches all seven.

Confusion

Confessing goes along with the idea of a certain confusion.

Momoyo Kaijima

Notes on Contemporary Landscape

Detour from the Detour

When I started studying architecture in university, I used to borrow all kinds of architecture books and magazines at random from the library, trying to find out what kind of architecture I wanted to make. I was intrigued by uniquely shaped architecture around the world illustrated in Architecture Without Architects by Bernard Rudofsky that indicated cultural and climatic differences and thought about the respective regions. Japan was experiencing the largest postwar economic bubble at that time and cities were overcrowded with postmodern buildings. I sympathized with those who went against the social trend and read books published by them, including *Introduction to Roadway Observation* by the ROJO Society (established by artist Genpei Akasegawa and architectural historian Terunobu Fujimori); *Tokyo: A Spatial Anthropology* by architectural historian Hidenori Jinnai, which compares waterfront spaces in Venezia and Edo (Tokyo), among others. I walked around the city every day to capture sights of architecture and urban legacy from the Edo and Meiji eras that were on the verge of disappearance, as well as new architecture. Daikanyama Dojunkai Apartments, which had been built as part of the disaster recovery construction after the Great Kanto Earthquake and reconstructed later as part of redevelopment, was one of my favorite places and I often visited the cafeteria for lunch and coffee. I became interested in cardboard box houses of homeless people staying at the Shinjuku Station concourse, observed and researched their life, while reading books on illegal occupation.

As for built works, I was drawn to architecture with a sense of incompleteness that indicates the state of uncompleted whole, self-build structures and open compositions. "Pioneer House" by Osamu Ishiyama. "Platform" by Kazuyo Sejima. "House F" by Kazunari Sakamoto. "Casa Bianchi" by Mario Botta. " Villa dall'Ava" by Rem Koolhaas. I liked the landscape where nature and the city flew into architecture.

Around that time, I obtained a copy of the SD (Japanese architecture magazine) May 1988 issue featuring Lucian Kroll. The front cover with a red background shows a photo of the house-shaped buildings at Technical

& Professional School in Belfort shot from a low angle. Wood shingle siding walls and 45-degree pitched roofs. Windows with red frames and aluminum frames are opened in the walls. An atmosphere of a traditional European house combined with factory-produced windows. It was a nostalgic and picturesque yet new and strange exterior landscape view to my eyes. The magazine features Kroll's works during 1980's after his breakthrough achievement of the Student Housing for Medical Faculty at the Catholic University of Louvain which had introduced Kroll's name to the world. At the Academy of Expression in Utrecht (1979), a theater was built in the courtyard with the participation of people. The roof is supported by arch-shaped plywood columns. A wood structural system that had been developed with the use of traditional agricultural techniques was constructed using factory-manufacturing methods. The next project, the Technical & Professional School in Belfort (1983–87), features a polyhedron roof with multiple windows installed at corners. The large-scale school building is composed of a repetition of small structural frames and various materials including shingles, metal sheets, slates and so on. While it almost looked like a city, it was also designed in such a way that allowed several small construction companies to collaborate and take part in the construction at the same time. Elementary School in Ciney (1983-86) and Elementary School in Saint Germain (1983–87) both have pleasant classrooms. Walls are located following the natural topography, and there is no square-shaped room. It seemed that the roofs echoing the complex topography and the windows bridging the roofs and walls provided cozy places for children who did not like going to school. Emerainville Apartments (1979–86) in Marne la Vallée aims to bring diversity to the town by placing factory-fabricated housing units around the courtyard based on opinions collected through dialogues with the residents. The approach way and wall finish of each apartment unit express the resident's personality. It reminded me of the unfettered and humorous renovation of Le Corbusier-designed apartments described in *Lived-In Architecture: Le Corbusier's Pessac Revisited* written by Phillippe Boudon I was reading at that time.

Kroll's works as a student, on the other hand, are filled with fragments of characteristic spatial elements in his architecture including the window, roof, stairs, terrace, greenery and so on. I could see, in his design studio work, the repetition of trial and error in an attempt to explore ways of designing architecture that would become part of a city.

One day, thirty years later, Jan de Vylder of advvt explained to me his plan for this booklet. When he asked me if I have architecture I should confess, the name of Lucien Kroll unexpectedly came to mind—perhaps somewhat influenced by the fact that Jan is a Belgian architect. After a moment of hesitation, I timidly confessed the name to Jan. He had a surprised look on his face for a moment, and said to me, "Sounds good. Let's do it."

Belgian Landscape

Belgium is a distant yet close country for me. The first thing associated with Belgium in my mind is a TV anime series "Dog of Flanders" (1974) based on a novel of the same name by English author Ouida that I watched as a five-year-old girl. It is a story about an impoverished boy who wanted to be a painter and his beloved dog in Flanders, Belgium. At the end of the story, the boy lost his grandfather (who was his only blood relative) by death, got disheartened by his failure in a painting contest, was too poor to eat, got separated from his beloved dog, and died in deep sadness and loneliness, in front of a Pieter Paul Rubens' painting in a cathedral. The dog found the dead boy and died due to sadness, lying next to him. While I was moved by the tragic ending, I was also fascinated by a landscape along a road where the boy walked to deliver milk cans. The flat landscape dotted with windmills in a Belgian farming village left a strong impression on me.

Later, as an adult, my friends and I frequently visited a Belgian beer bar in Tokyo. The bar was always very dimly lit, because the owner paid particular attention to keep it dark. One day I opened my laptop computer and he immediately told me to close it because the screen was too bright for the darkness of the room. The bar had such a distinct atmosphere.

I started visiting Belgium on business over a decade ago. The purpose for visit was a lecture, exhibition, building project and so on and I visited not only urban areas but also a former mining town in a severe economic situation which was redeveloped into a new center of the IT industry. I visited Antwerp for a meeting with our clients, and was intrigued to hear them speak a random mixture of Flemish and French in daily conversations. During the visit I stopped by a beer bar that was even darker than the bar in Tokyo. Interestingly, I have observed random collages of buildings in different styles, classes, and scales along the streets in all of the cities I visited. It seems that ornaments and unique shapes are accepted there. While some of the buildings are adorned with cast iron ornaments reminiscent of the golden days of the cast iron industry, industrial products including aluminum components are actively used in many buildings. The way the old and new, as well as the darkness and light, coexist in these cities overlaps with the image of the vivid interaction between the distinct light and people in the paintings of Pieter Paul Rubens and Pieter Bruegel in my mind's eye.

One weekend in March 2019, Jan, photographer Filip Dujardin, and I made a trip to visit the Student Housing for Medical Faculty at the Catholic University of Louvain. Our plan was to take a train from Brussels

Airport, transfer to another train at Brussels Station, and arrive at Alma Station located in the center of the Kroll's student building. Jan kindly gave me detailed commentaries on architecture and cities. For example Brussels Station, where we transferred, designed by Victor Horta, seemed that all spatial components, including the hall, platforms, underground paths, and stairs were designed to celebrate the space in the then new station building. It is beautifully designed, full of warm feelings, composed of yellow tiles, light fixtures and handrails in brass and so on. As soon as the train left the station, we saw a view of the red light district around the station scattered with shops with indecent names through the window. After a while, a beautiful rural landscape dotted with houses with 45-degree-angled pitched roofs spread in front of our eyes outside the window. I looked closely and spotted various structures including greenhouses and small sheds with tin or wooden roofs that the residents had built by themselves in the backyards. It occurred to me that distinct scenes I had observed in Kroll's works might have originated in this landscape, and my expectations for the building we were visiting rose. Meanwhile, the train arrived at Alma Station.

Landscape at the Student Housing for Medical Faculty at the Catholic University of Louvain

I actually felt a little lost when we got off the train, because I couldn't locate myself in the building even though I had thoroughly studied the plan in advance. The station, although located above-ground, was covered with a concrete roof and rather dark. Part of finish materials on the polygonal ceiling were coming off and the concrete slab and rough beams were exposed through the gap. The concrete columns supporting the roof were leaf-shaped, which seemed to me like a rather abrupt expression. Jan explained to me that perhaps some ideas of landscape architect Simone Kroll, Lucien Kroll's wife, might have been incorporated. I secretly wondered if this was going to be like a disappointing reunion with one's first love after thirty years. Seeing the troubled look on my face, Jan got worried and suggested that we take a walk.

After we went out of the station and walked around, I realized that the building was under renovation after fifty years. The organization managing the renovation work had their own space in the gallery next to the station, and the walls were covered with drawings showing the renovation process and posters of related events. We followed the side street to get to the other side of the station, passed through a building, and finally arrived in front of the famous façade of the Kroll's building. I felt relieved to see the familiar view with the unique assemblage of various windows.

We started our building tour from there. We went up the stairs to the terrace that connects to the second and third floors, from which we were able to take a closer look at the various windows. Various types of windows, including fixed windows with dark-brown wooden frames, inward-opening windows with red frames, and sliding windows with aluminum frames are installed as necessary in an ad-hoc manner, and the surfaces next to the windows are finished with aluminum curtain walls. Some parts of the exterior walls are exposed, while the other parts are finished with materials including slate, shingles, and steel sheet. Jan explained me that this is a typical insulation/finish construction method of brick walls in Belgium. Handrails, made of diagonally cut C-shaped steel channel to drain rainwater, are bolted to the edge of the slab and wood boards are installed horizontally. The stairs at the end of the terrace go up almost to the top floor. Handrails on the upper floors are made of steel and covered with a net. It seems that the exterior stairs are not only used for internal circulation but also as evacuation stairs.

There is a roof garden following the undulation of the roof of the station building, where flowers and rosemary are planted and people can freely stroll around. The roof and partially attached fish scale-shaped polycarbonate eaves, perhaps intended to be used as stalls, surround the plaza.

Another student building across the courtyard has a stair hall covered with a glass roof, and two large monuments respectively in the shape of a man and a woman stand there. People pass by the monuments and go up the stairs to access different wings of the student housing. The stairs are composed of stacks of sturdy C-shaped precast concrete pieces, and exposed concrete walls on both sides of the stairs welcome people with the vivid color created by applying multiple paint coats. Corners of access doors on piping shafts are rounded. Roughness and delicacy coexist in this space.

In another student housing, deep terraces seemed to serve as a main circulation route. We went up to a terrace and met foreign students from Africa, who apparently use terraces to visit each other's room. The glass-clad greenhouse on the top floor is equipped with a shared kitchen, decorated with national flags and posters, with boxes full of empty beer bottles lying around—a familiar "after-party" scene in a student housing. The ground floor and lower floors accommodate public facilities including a bar, cafe, kindergarten, elementary school, university offices, church and so on. A chorus group was practicing in the church. Public facilities were closed for the weekend, but it seemed that many of them were still actively used fifty years later.

The renovation work of the station building included an addition of new elevators providing access to the roof and terraces. The new design seemed to inherit some of the typical "Kroll" design features including the details of the existing blue stair handrails and the undulated roof on the elevator tower. Lucien Kroll, now over 90 years old, and his colleagues still retain their atelier, and I suppose they may be supervising or giving advice regarding the student housing. I was very glad to be given the opportunity to see this landscape where the fifty-year-old building was still under construction and actively used today.

After walking around the campus for about two hours, I looked at the entire building from a distance, some distance away from the kindergarten playground, and discovered that the outline of the building was shaped like a large roof. Because the building is composed of miscellaneous materials and discontinuous shapes including the terraces, the large roof-like shape looked more like a mountain than a roof. Come to think of it, the fact I felt lost and did not know what to focus on when I arrived at the station—it might have been exactly what Kroll intended. Perhaps I was looking at "architecture as landscape" that Kroll aimed to create—suddenly, it made sense to me.

Landscape through a Gap

After that, we went back to Brussels, visited an art museum designed by Horta, and headed to Gent where Jan and his partners are based. Jan and I visited three buildings designed by advvt.

We visited "PC Caritas" first. It is a multipurpose pavilion located on a hospital campus converted from a former mansion house property on the outskirts of Gent. They removed roofs and windows, preserved brick walls and part of floors in the existing buildings on the property, and converted them into a three-dimensional park where patients can engage in various activities during pleasant seasons. Generally, hospitals are painted white and required to maintain a high level of cleanliness to fight diseases, but both patients and medical staff often feel suffocated in such environment. At PC Caritas, the brick walls are exposed, the roof was removed to let in light, wind, and rain, and trees are integrated as part of the building. A newly built greenhouse, nested within the semi-exterior space, is used for workshops and events. The existing fireplace was revived and put to use. The building, converted through careful subtractions of existing components, cannot be fully enclosed, but that is exactly why it serves as a special place to protect people's wellbeing—a kind of place which doesn't exist in typical hospitals.

Next, we visited a clothing store "onderbergen" located in the city center of Gent. One of the bay windows in the white-painted brick building was removed and re-installed as a "reversed bay window" protruding inward. As a result, the wall and the window started to behave in different ways: a "double-void" combining a "void" of an existing window

Momoyo Kaijima

Lucien Kroll
La Mémé

Filip Dujardin

June 14, 2019

FOOD
TRAMINOT
BAR
TRAMINOT

M

CENTRE
OECUMENIQUE
KAP CONTES

Inge Vinck

Drawing for Lucien. For Momoyo

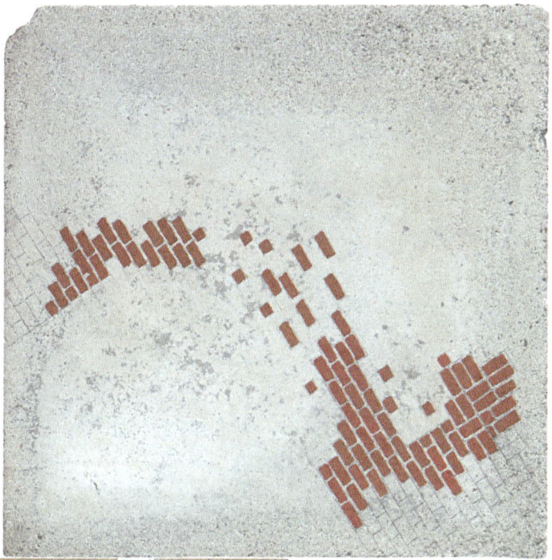

Momoyo Kaijima

Through Belgian Gaps

SD 88 05

【特集】

ルシアン・クロール

自由・冒険・挑戦：ルシアン・クロールの建築世界

The Architecture of Lucien Kroll: Freedom, Adventure, Challenge

【作品】

ユトレヒトの演劇学校

マルヌ・ラ・ヴァレのエムランヴィル集合住宅

セルジ・ポントワースのヴィーネ・ブランシュ集合住宅　ほか

【座談会】

澤田誠二＋重村力＋玄・ベルトー・進来

ワークショップ

Nine Works by WORKSHOP

【文】吉見俊哉

SSN 0563-0991
ースデザイン都市・建築・芸術の総合誌
284号昭和63年5月1日発行毎月1回1日発行
和40年2月5日第3種郵便物認可

Alma

根スまつうばり製さトで

屋ラのるの選く坂持ッ漏

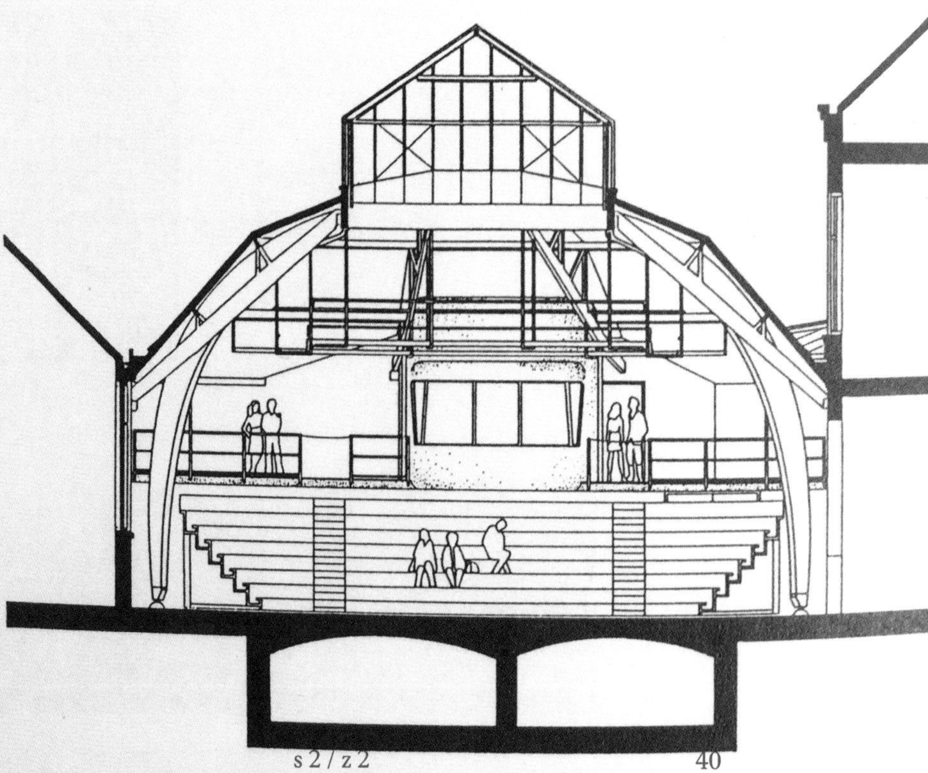

工事中のスナップ．　中庭に屋根を架ける．

ÉCOLE

スケッチ

建物はパブリック・スクエアをとり囲むグループごとに考えられている。　各住宅に至るアプローチは，通りから，裏側から，外部階段から，あるいは隣りの住宅のファサードについている階段からといった具合に，おのおのが独立したものとして計画された。

DE KASTART

opening in the wall and a new "void" generated by the inwardly protruding window connects spaces (inside and outside) in different ways from the original building envelope.

Lastly, we visited "43", advvt's conversion of a vacant house purchased by an artist in an industrial workers' residential district clustered with row houses made of brick. The existing structure is the artist's residence and the annex in the back across the courtyard is her atelier. They installed a sliding roof over the courtyard so that it can be used as both interior and exterior spaces. The existing house has four floors. Firstly, they made a hole in the wall to make straight stairs from the ground floor to the first floor, and fold-up stairs are installed to connect the two loft floors above.

These architectural works by advvt create new relationships between inside/outside as well as between different layers by re-editing architectural elements including the roof, window, stairs, and greenery, which were notable features in Kroll's architecture. By doing so, advvt physically and semantically created "gaps" in their architecture, and I was able to see a landscape I had never seen before through these gaps.

Landscape through the eyes of Kroll and advvt

Coincidentally, this booklet project gave me an opportunity to visit Kroll's architecture and advvt's architecture in one day. Jan told me that some people have drawn comparisons between them, but they are not particularly conscious about that when they design. I think it is true. But through the eyes of a person coming from a distant country of Japan, architecture of both architects seemed to present architectural solutions to the "two-sidedness" unique to cities and villages in Belgium. It is about the relationship between the "facade" of a main building and the "courtyard" and/or "backyard" behind it. The "facade" is expected to engage with society, and masonry wall facades (most typical in Belgium) are designed to indicate the status of respective buildings by the type of material, style, or construction method used. On the other hand, courtyards and backyards were originally common spaces equipped with public wells in the center and shared among buildings and people around them, and they were later privatized due to the modernization of utility infrastructure. For this reason, when one's life exceeds the limit of the main building and overflows into the courtyard and backyard, he/she starts building a greenhouse and shed by himself/herself while incorporating prefabricated products in ad-hoc manners. Thus, landscape of free life spread throughout the country. The landscape in Kroll's architecture is the result of developing relationships between people and architecture that are similar to relationships between people and architecture in the courtyards and backyards in the Belgian landscape throughout architecture during the first industrialization. Fifty years later, architecture has largely been industrialized and the meaning of “inside” and “outside” is becoming more ambiguous beyond the physical boundary in contemporary society. In contrast, advvt's architecture cuts through the existing landscape by applying the methods seen in the courtyards and backyards in the Belgian landscape. Landscapes seen in their architecture are free spaces made possible by freeing architecture from the ambiguous relationships. These spaces are the results of daily endeavors, not only by architects but also by clients and residents who materialize and operate architecture, to go beyond the existing relationship between people and architecture. This kind of collaboration between architects and residents has much in common with the culture of post-war Japan where a large number of private houses were built through collaboration between architects and clients. Both Kroll and advvt, fifty years apart, have been fighting against ossification of architecture due to industrialization and striving to maintain the link between architecture, society and culture.

I would like to look at the landscape in Japan in comparison to this. While the landscape in Japan does not indicate clear contrasts such as the "facade and courtyard", Japan had built cities and settlements with highly elaborate culture underpinned by its unique wood construction techniques. However, due to modernization, urbanization, earthquake disaster reconstruction, and war damage reconstruction, Japan was forced to build an incredible number of buildings. As a result, contemporary architecture in Japan could not help relying on the construction industry which had expanded greatly. Due to restrictions on building specifications imposed by urban densification and environmental issues, the change of building materials from wood to steel and concrete has been handled solely based on functions without achieving the same level of high architecture culture in the past, and as a matter of fact, landscapes in cities and villages have lost rich qualities they had in the past and are becoming more and more ossified today. Under such circumstances, Atelier Bow-Wow called out to everyone to rediscover urban "gaps" in Tokyo, in order to focus on environments around buildings that existed outside the realm of architecture tied to the construction industry. Focusing on gaps is a movement to reevaluate the ecological and interactive relationships architecture has been developing for a long time, reincorporate architecture as a creative existence, and use it as a tool to continuously engage with the culture and society in our life. Just like Kroll and advvt, I keep exploring ways to break the trend of architectural ossification in Japan. This trip made me realize again that the challenges continuing over thirty years in the distant yet close country of Belgium have been encouraging me to continue my way as an architect like a cheering song. Thank you, Jan.

Maarten Delbeke

Indifference and Denial

One of the several texts by Belgian architecture critic Geert Bekaert on the architect of la Mémé is entitled "Lucien Kroll en de verloochening van de architectuur" – Lucien Kroll and the denial of architecture. Published in 1968, the article offers a brief analysis of three projects Kroll built right before the Mémé: a housing compound in Oudergem (B), a religious center in Chevigny (B), and what Bekaert calls "building in Africa," a long term housing project in Rwanda. Bekaert explains his interest in Kroll by stating that his work "is afraid to be architecture." Kroll's architecture, so Bekaert writes, "excels in a simple sense of reality." It appears to locate its raison d'être in the inhabitant or user, not in the formal requirements of the architecture itself or the ambitions of its designer. In Bekaert's view, the examples discussed in the article attest to Kroll's capacity to rethink the process of designing and building to give shape to the conditions of life.

Bekaert's assessment of Kroll would become increasingly negative over the course of his writing career, to the point that Kroll came to embody much of what Bekaert loathed in certain kinds of contemporary architecture. In the pages Bekaert devoted to Kroll in his Contemporary architecture in Belgium (1995), the Mémé is cast "as the perfect simulacrum of architecture that pretends to be what architecture is not and will never be." Bekaert voices his irritation about Kroll's simulation of spontaneity and participation while meticulously designing the entire building, and his celebration of prefabrication as a means to liberate the creativity of workers and users only to particularise every aspect of the building. On top of this, Bekaert accuses Kroll of attributing social and even political meaning to his formal preoccupations, under the guise of a supposed denial of the prerogatives of the architect. In Bekaert's view, Kroll's evocation of tradition is a myth, his genius loci a fabrication.

Geert Bekaert was a towering figure in architectural criticism in Flanders and the Netherlands from the 1950s until his death in 2015. His work is very much predicated on the conditions of architectural practice in Belgium. Until the 1990s, an exceptional degree of legal protection of the architect's profession there was paired with a *laissez-faire* attitude to all matters involving urban planning and architectural policy, to stunning effect on the built environment. Every building potentially became a statement—architectural or other—within an unregulated urbanized landscape. In this setting, Kroll's strategy of celebrating bottom-up creativity under the firm control of the designer appears as a disingenuous engagement with the conditions of production of the built environment, celebrating and exploiting the freedom afforded to potentially any builder only in name. Bekaert was profoundly irritated by Kroll's blend of ostentation and humility, which dissimulates architectural ambition under the guise of political engagement. In Bekaert's view, rarely does architecture act up as much as it does in this case. We are made to look at a piece of magic, dazzled into believing that there is nothing to see. It takes other architects—not builders, users, inhabitants—to recognize the sophistication of what is on offer; ultimately, despite its pretense, this architecture talks about architecture to architects.

Bekaert's disavowal of Kroll helps to explain the awkward position of Kroll's work in general, and the Mémé in particular, in the collective architectural consciousness of the Low Countries. Also, no other 20th-century Belgian oeuvre has been perceived so differently across the country's linguistic divide, with general—if certainly not universal—disapproval on the Flemish side and a much more welcoming reception in Wallonia. Finally, as Bekaert himself acknowledges, the disparity between Kroll's international fame and his national reputation is enormous. As this very publication illustrates, the Mémé in particular has been promoted in the international architectural press, and it figures in surveys of postmodern architecture. No doubt Kroll's canonisation was aided by its easy classification under such monikers as participatory architecture, and Kroll himself was as much at home in the European architectural scene as in Belgium. Kroll himself has built an extensive international oeuvre.

Is this discrepancy because some matters could only be recognized and valued in a different context than Belgium? Is there something myopic about Bekaert's disavowal? Perhaps, but there is more to it than an excessive preoccupation with the plights of Belgian architecture. Bekaert's entire written oeuvre, and indeed his attitude towards Belgian architecture, is predicated on a very strong idea of 'architecture,' an idea that stands in diametric opposition to the oeuvre of Kroll. In Bekaert's view, architecture is at once existential and superfluous, depending on how one situates it in reality. On a fundamental level, humankind requires architecture to structure its existence, literally by delineating places in an otherwise infinite reality, metaphorically by structuring language and thought. At the same time, architecture understood as a practice and a profession eternally fails to give form to this fundamental need, as it loses itself in gratuitous play or offers no resistance to the forces it is supposed to structure. Only architects—for it is they who produce 'architecture', in Bekaert's view—aware of the profound incapacity of their work to fully encompass its remit, are worthy of that name. In their work buildings do not just occupy, represent or mould a place for living, but they also hint at the possibilities and limits of human existence.

This position explains Bekaert's fundamental disagreement with Kroll. In this view, an architecture that seeks to mimic the very life it should accommodate is doomed to failure. But it is worth asking what the alternative is. In the case of Kroll this alternative is joined at the hip with its counterpart. Between 1951 and 1957 Kroll collaborated with Charles Vandenhove, with whom he had studied. Like Kroll, Vandenhove would build an extensive oeuvre in Belgium, but more so outside it. But unlike Kroll, and very much in line with Bekaert's critical judgment, Vandenhove has been canonized as a key figure in Belgian post-war architecture.

The antithesis between Kroll and Vandenhove is perhaps just one version of a duality that runs through the last century of architectural history. Both Kroll and Vandenhove were critical of modernism and explored themes of tectonics, the vernacular and habitat in their joint works. But in contrast to Kroll, Vandenhove chose to develop an architectural idiom rooted in geometry, basic forms and, progressively, references to the classical tradition. In the view of Bekaert and many who have followed his lead, this approach has led the way to an architecture that is at once present and distant, clear but obscure, legible yet open to interminable interpretation. In other words, an architecture that at once hints at its existential core while making room for life. Geometry, volumetry and history are means of mediating between these two poles, at once affirming an identity of architecture—its autonomy, if you like—while refusing to take the place of life itself.

If this position has the merit of consistency, it also outlines a very specific critical position. It is lenient towards the often excruciating formalism of, for instance, Vandenhove's work, and relies on a very specific idea of what architecture can and should mean to society. Perhaps this meaning is best summarized with the notion of indifference. As an ex-Jesuit, Bekaert would have been profoundly familiar with this concept, as it is foundational to Jesuit spirituality. There, it underpins any truthful engagement with the world: the capacity to forfeit anything, even that which is dearest to oneself, which does not contribute to loving God or others. Indifference quite closely resembles what Bekaert expects architecture to be: fully and completely engaged with reality, yet ready at any moment to step back and accept its inability to transform reality itself. Conversely, indifference is what Bekaert expects us to feel for architecture: an unending cycle of almost greedy enthusiasm that is forfeited once we recognize how it diverts us from a more essential truth, or enshrined when we feel it encapsulates such truth. This forced denial is difficult to envision in the face of Kroll's architecture. It works itself into our consciousness, to an irritating degree. This imposition may be highly problematic from many points of view, but it also forces us out of the comfort zone that indifference allows us—architects, critics, historians—to establish.

carrousel
confessions
confusion

Carrousel

Carrousel was first an exhibition at ETH advvt held in 2015. The exhibition was divided in three parts. One was about seven interventions in the space of the gta. One was about showing the work of almost forty Belgian architects we liked; revealing through this selection ourselves, our interests, our attitude. One was about showing our own work; we decided to show in the cabinet, behind the wooden wall. Carrousel setting ran for one year, hosting other exhibitions by gta. Each the same yet different. Every exhibition leaving a trace.

Carrousel is now the furniture of our office at ETH, since we arrived in summer 2017. We cut the wall in pieces and we arranged tables, bookshelves, archive, paravents. Together with some of the furnitures of the following exhibitions that took place in the setting we made for the gta. Office kgdvs' bistro chairs, Shinohara's white tables, Dan Graham's sofa. Working with the existing things, catching traces, collecting objects.

Carrousel is going to be a series of books. Again revealing both our colleagues' personal interests and our own.

In the form of confessions.

Confessions

Confessing is something personal.

Confessions are about
something embarrassing or confusing
love, at least for a moment
something abandoned or refurbished
something which is not a sign of the times
something badly published or not at all
something not easy to clean
something we do not know much about

and if you do not find anything that matches any of these rules
you can choose one of your works
that is embarrassing
or
that matches all seven.

Confusion

Confessing goes along with the idea of a certain confusion.

Inge Vinck

Holidays

Family house, Menthon St Bernard.

It all begins in 1997 when I discover the work of Patrice Mottini, one of my diploma professors at St Lucas Ghent.

I must admit, I first fall in love with his school of architecture in Rouen. The renovation with the gentle and ingenious structural solutions and details. The wonderful golden stairs.
But also the extension with a new building. Classrooms in the trees. And a conference space without finishing the plasterboards, or is it finished! All I can say, it is intriguing.

And there is the primary school *Les Retentis*, which I have never had the chance to visit, and unfortunately I will never have, as it has been demolished recently.

After finishing my studies I begin working in the office of Patrice Mottini in Paris. My first job, I am still somewhat naïve, just discovering what architecture and detailing is about. And

what it means to a building. The importance of materials. More specifically, in the office I learn to understand the importance of drawing. Patrice is always drawing with his pen. Jalil Amor—a collaborator—with paint, the photocopier, pencils, whatever; always very colorful; making paintings and collages of details, interiors, buildings. Both drawing with a lot of passion, as research for the development of a project, and as research into the materials, colors, details, moments.

In 1999, Patrice's office is selected for competition for a square in Annecy.
Patrice invites me to spend the summer holidays in the family house near Annecy, to work on the competition. The family house has been one of his first projects. Patrice made his first sketches in 1970, after having finished his studies.

So it happens that in August I am waiting for a train to Annecy at Gare de Lyon in Paris, to go to the house in Menthon St Bernard. I arrive during the night, which is a pity. Patrice told me so often about the scenic approach to the house. An experience that I will finally discover the next day.

I arrive and find myself suddenly part of the family. During summertime the whole family meets in the house. The house is built for the family to live together. Every family has their own space but in between, everyone meets. On the stairs. In the different smaller and bigger areas

Tartiflette (Annecy)   beau-frère Patrice Mottini

pommes de terre
aile
lardons
Reblochon
lait

faites cuire les pommes de terre
dans plat : un mélange d'ail et de lait
rajoutez les pommes de terres (coupées)
et les lardons
recouvrez avec des plaques de Reblochon
mettez dans le four, jusqu'à ce que
le fromage soit "bien" fondu.

with seats or tables. On the pallier. But most of the time in the kitchen, to eat lunch and dinner together.
The tartiflette made by Patrice's brother is still one of my favorites. I still make it now and then, but during winter as to me it is more of a winter dish.
Every morning at 8am we go for an early morning swim in the fresh water of lake Annecy. Wonderful moments, with the lake and the mountains behind it.

During my stay I would walk around at different moments of the day to enjoy the house and its details. The gutters, the technical shafts, the brickwork, the supporting elements of the beams, the structural details, the colors, the volumes. I looked around me and discovered. Everything was fascinating; life in the house, the living together, the tiny spaces and the larger spaces, the corners, the light, the views, the tiny colorful bathrooms, the many stairs.
I enjoyed and undoubtedly fell in love with this house.

The perfect environment to make the first drawings and sketches for a competion.

But most of all a nice stay.
In a beautiful, inspiring house.

Inge Vinck

Patrice Mottini Family House

Filip Dujardin

November 12, 2017

Inge Vinck

Drawing for Patrice

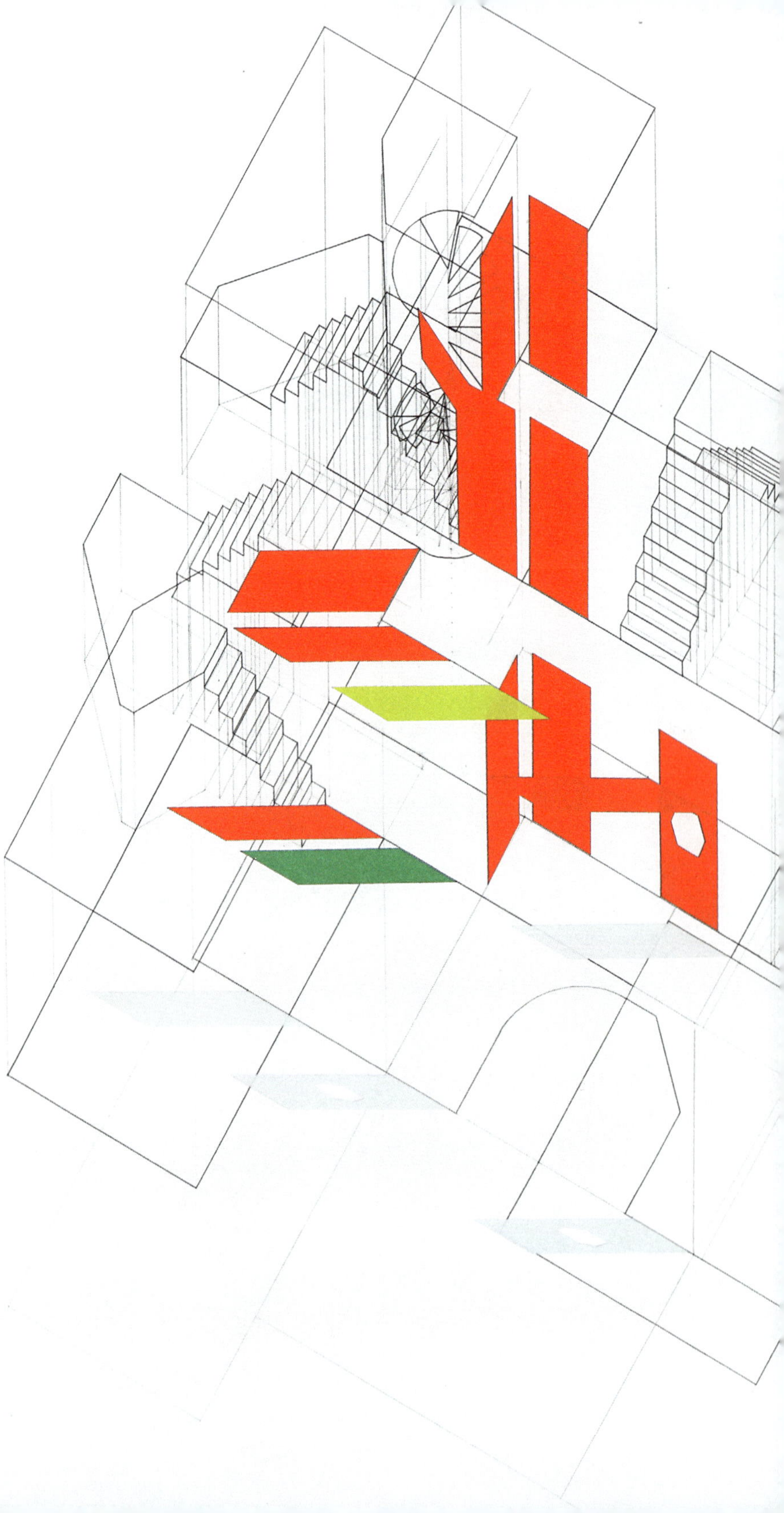

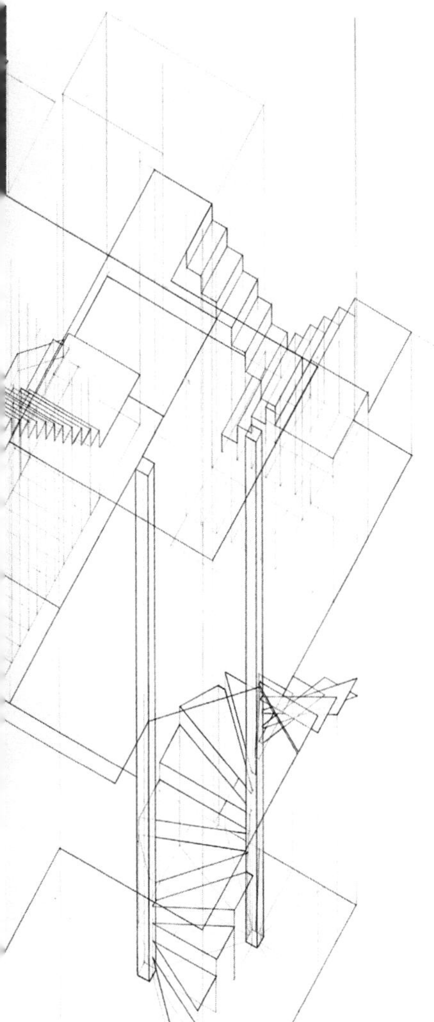

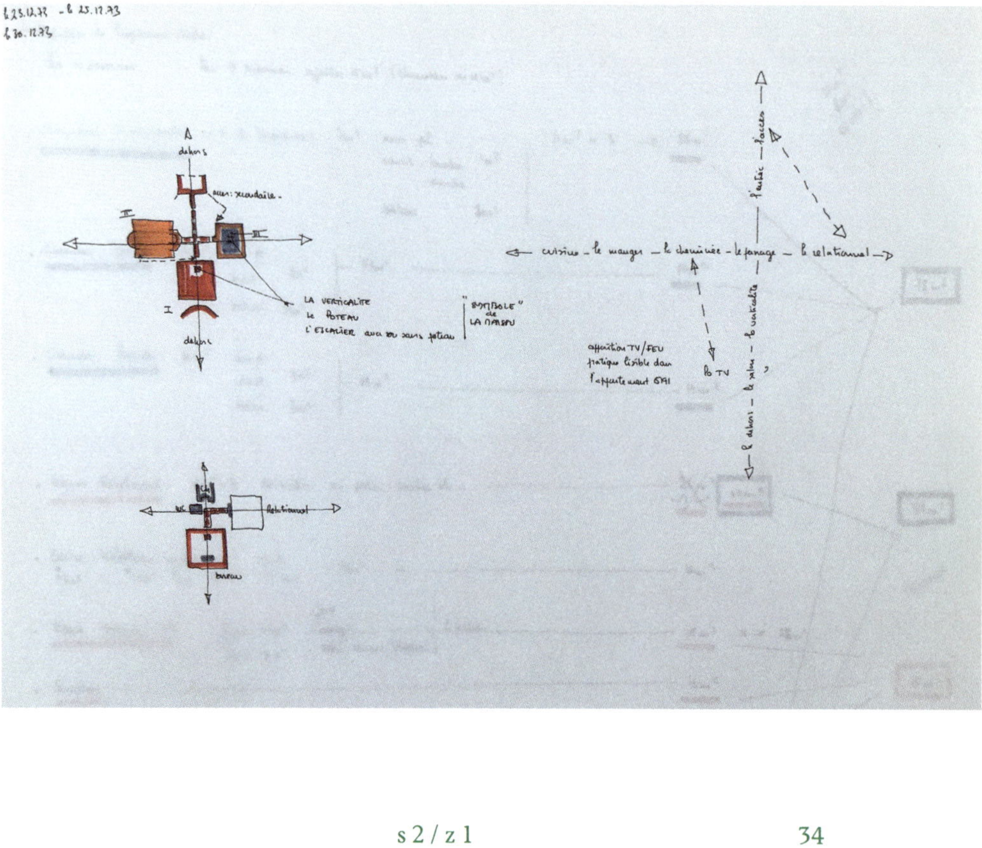
dehors
LA VERTICALITE
le POTEAU
dehors

Inge Vinck

Esquisse

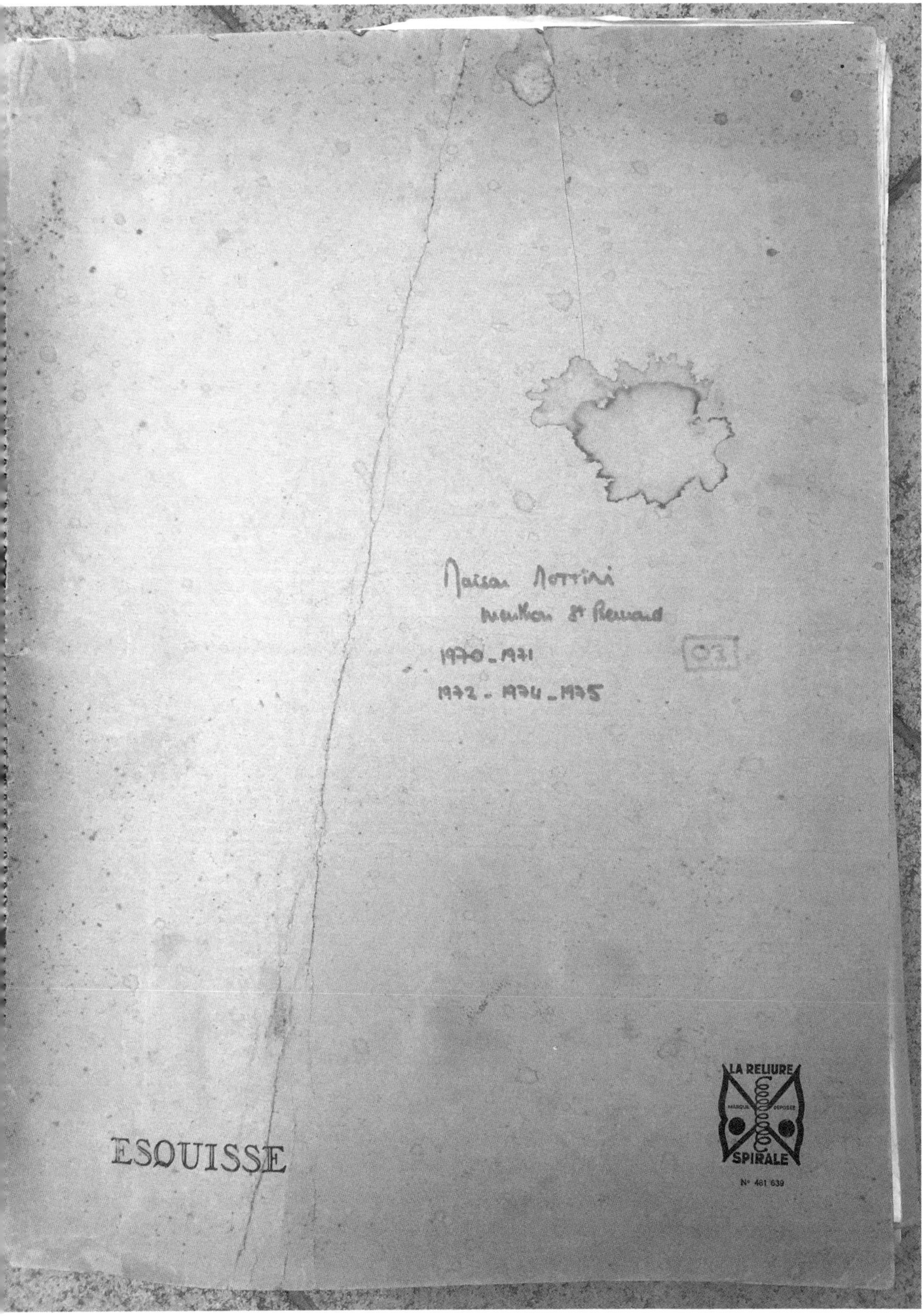
Maison Rottini
Menthon St Bernard
1970_1971
1972_1974_1975
ESQUISSE
LA RELIURE
MARQUE DÉPOSÉE
SPIRALE
N° 481 639

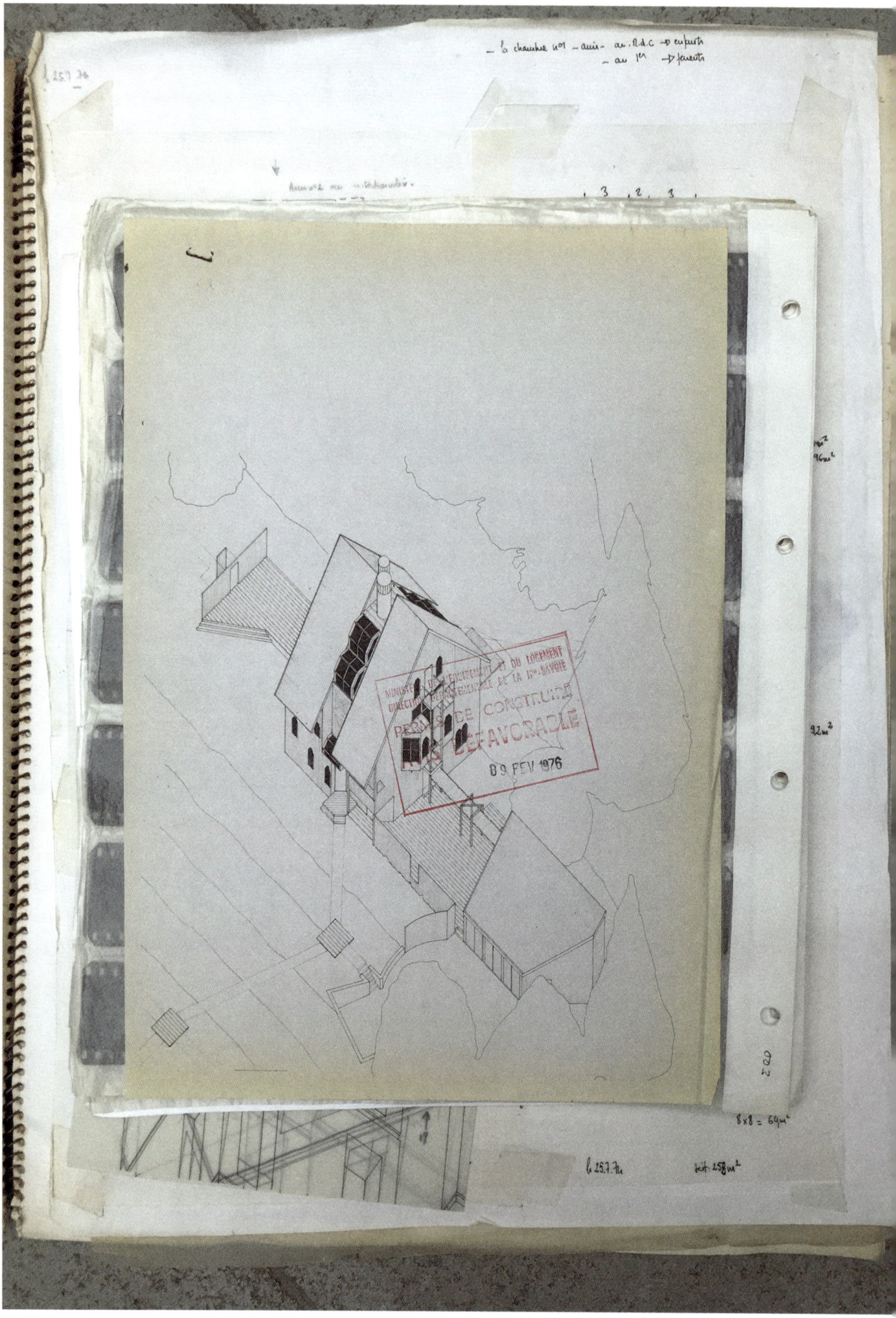

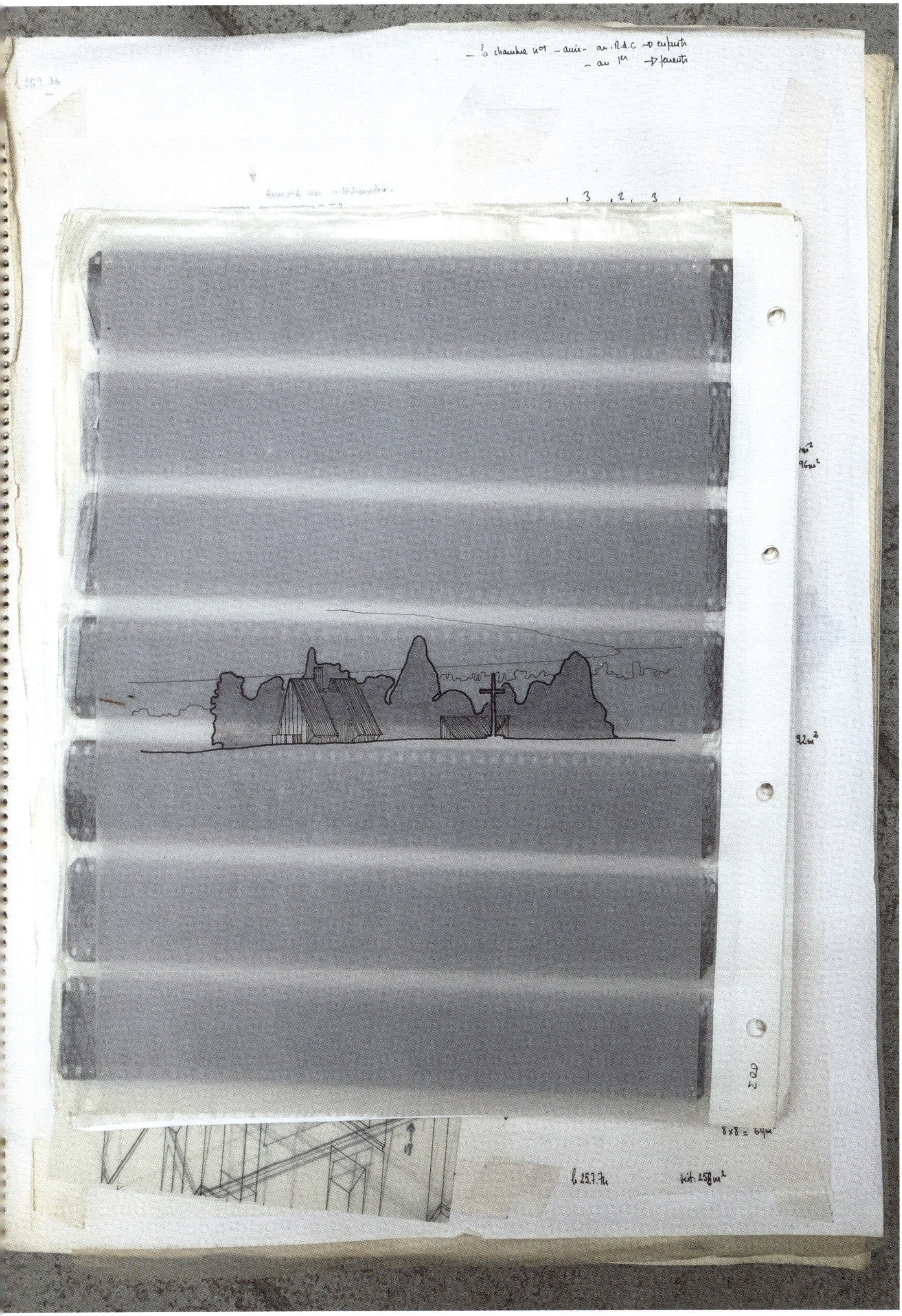

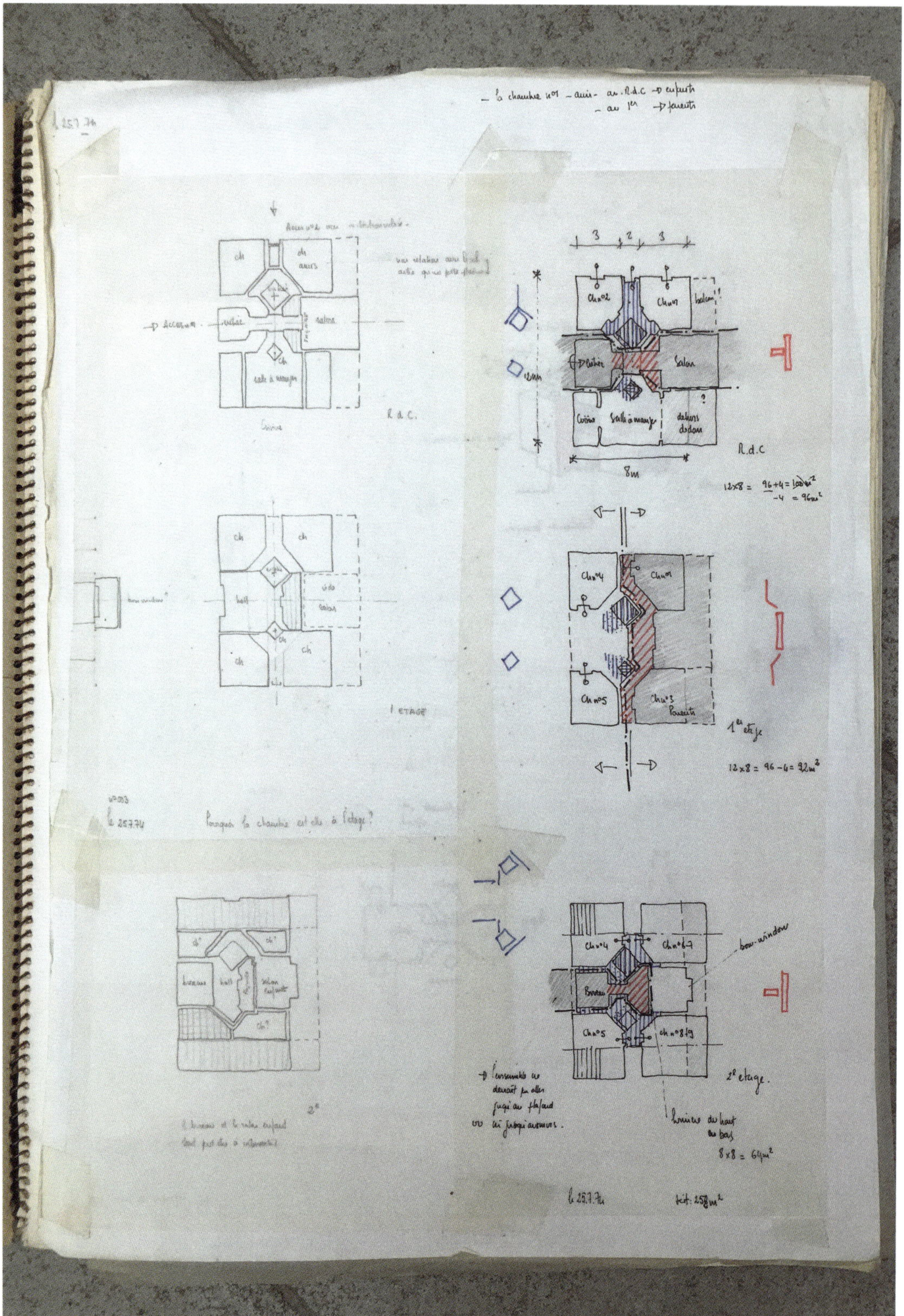

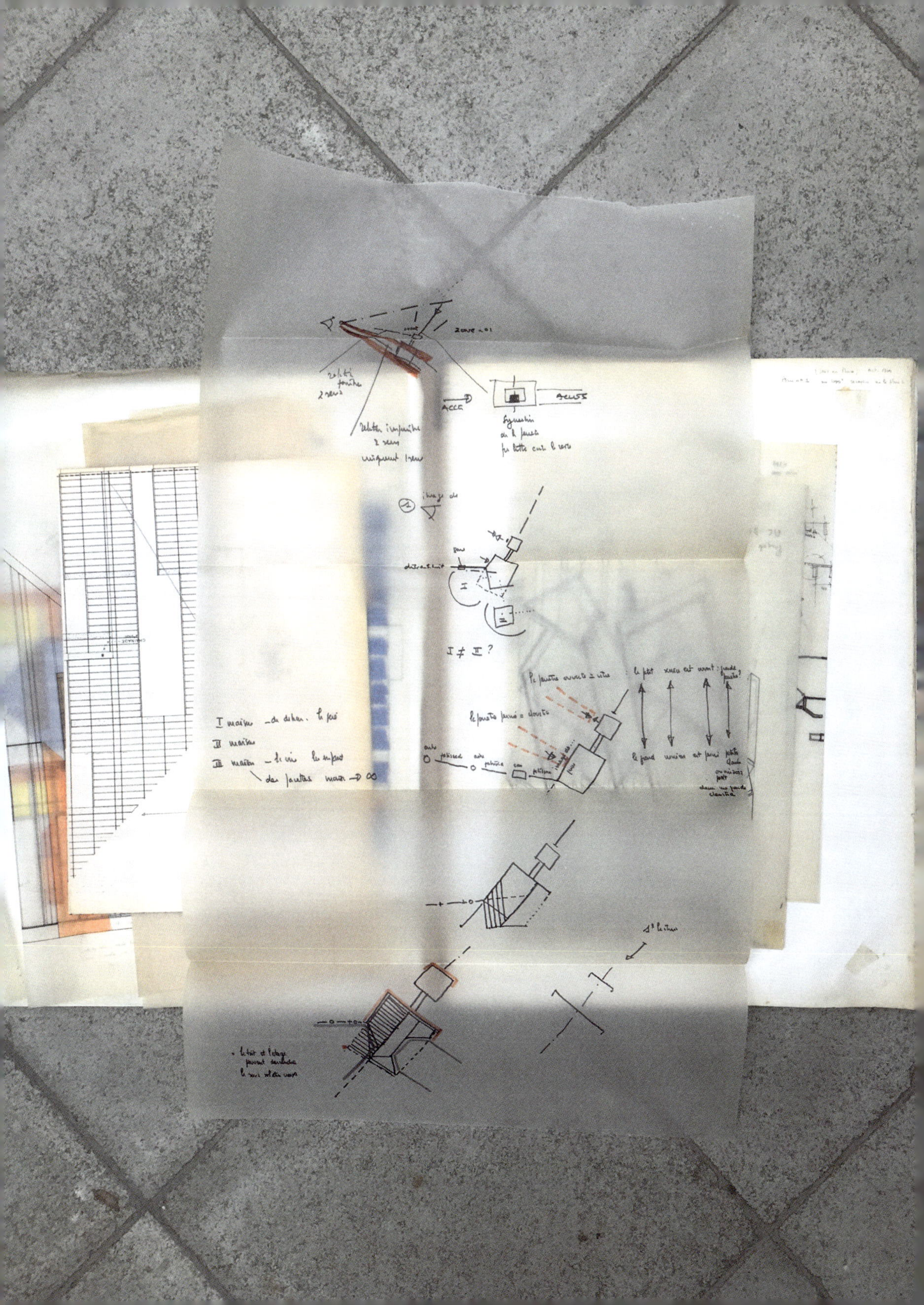

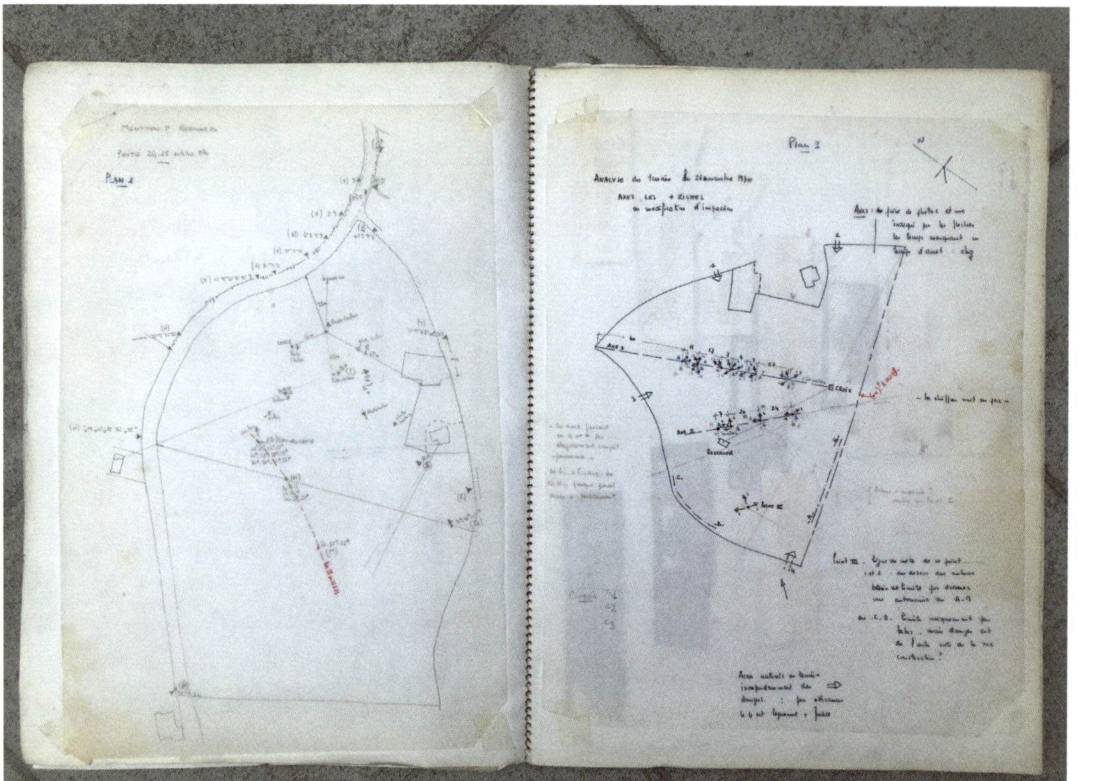

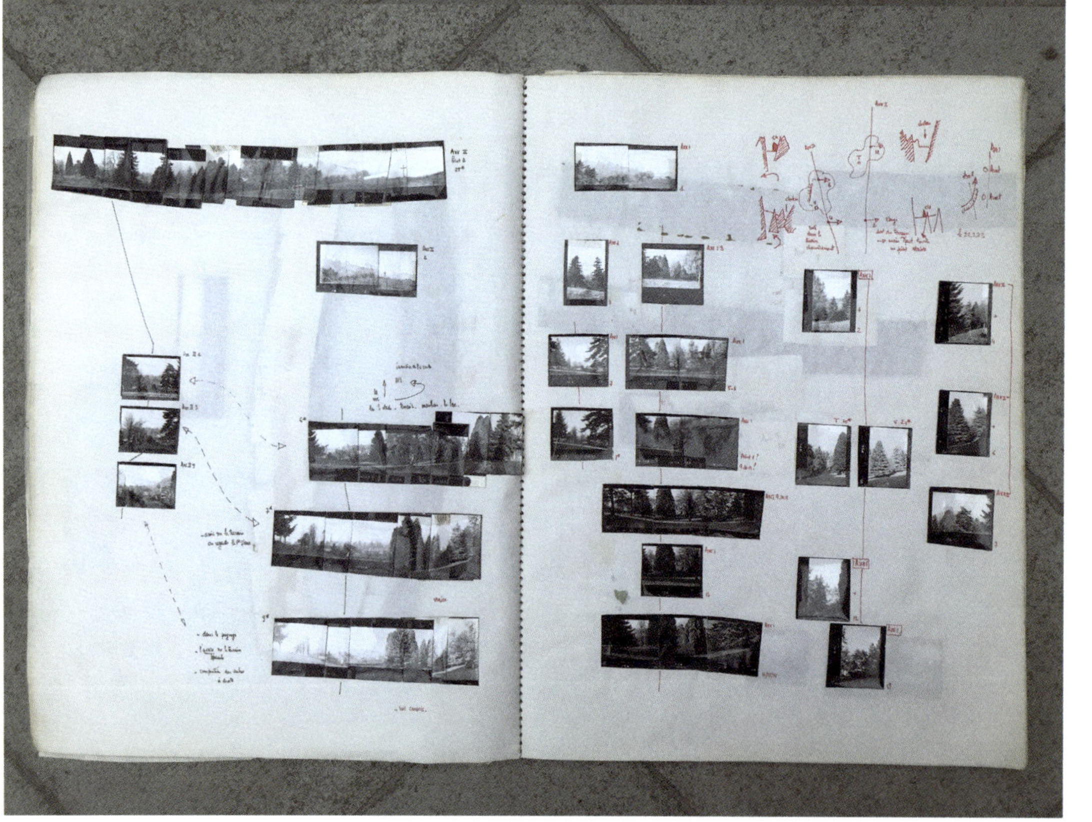

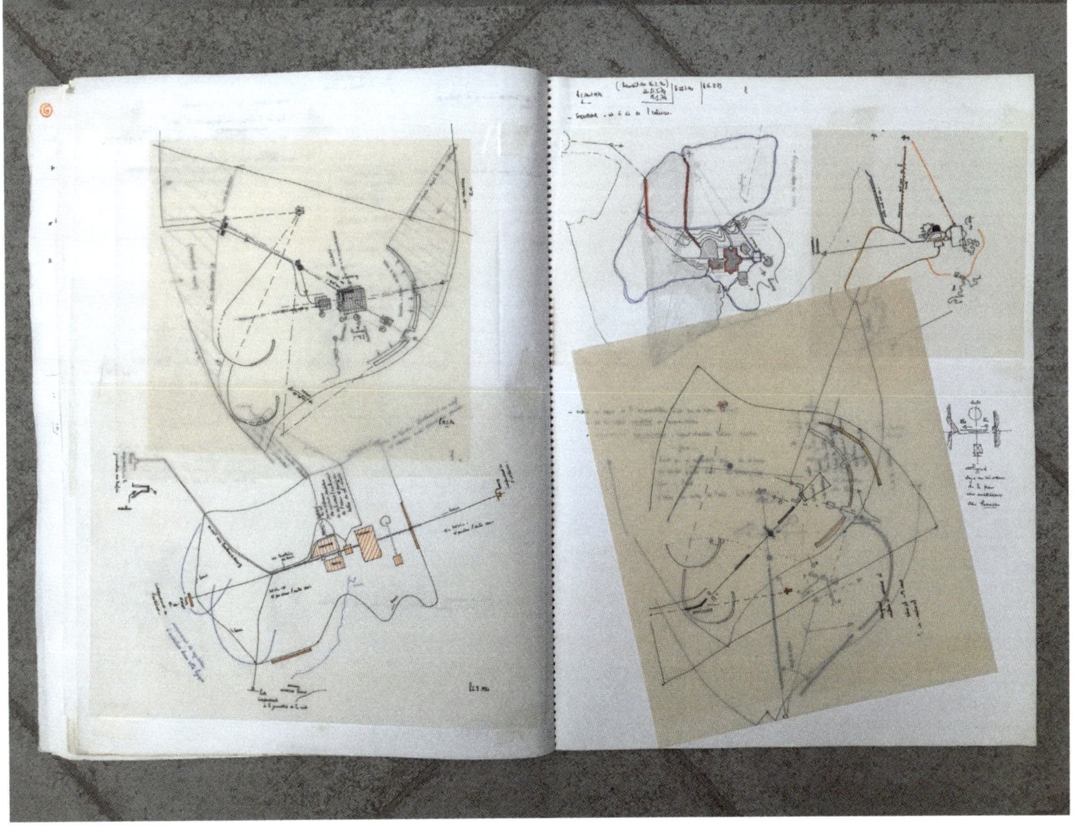

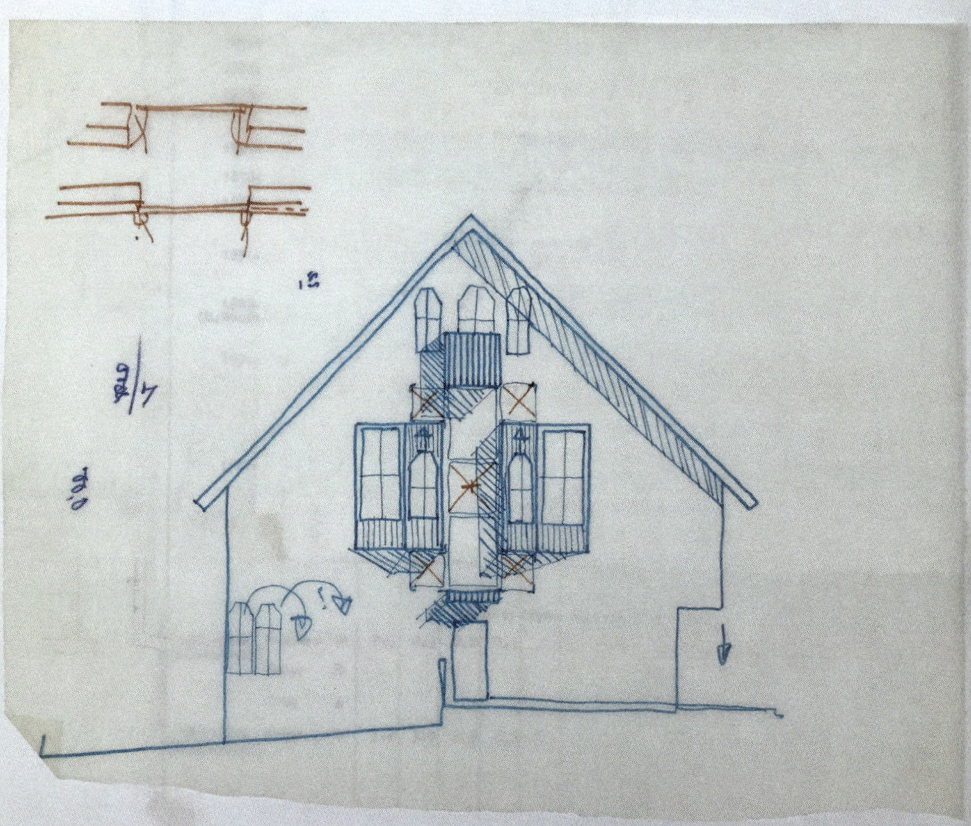

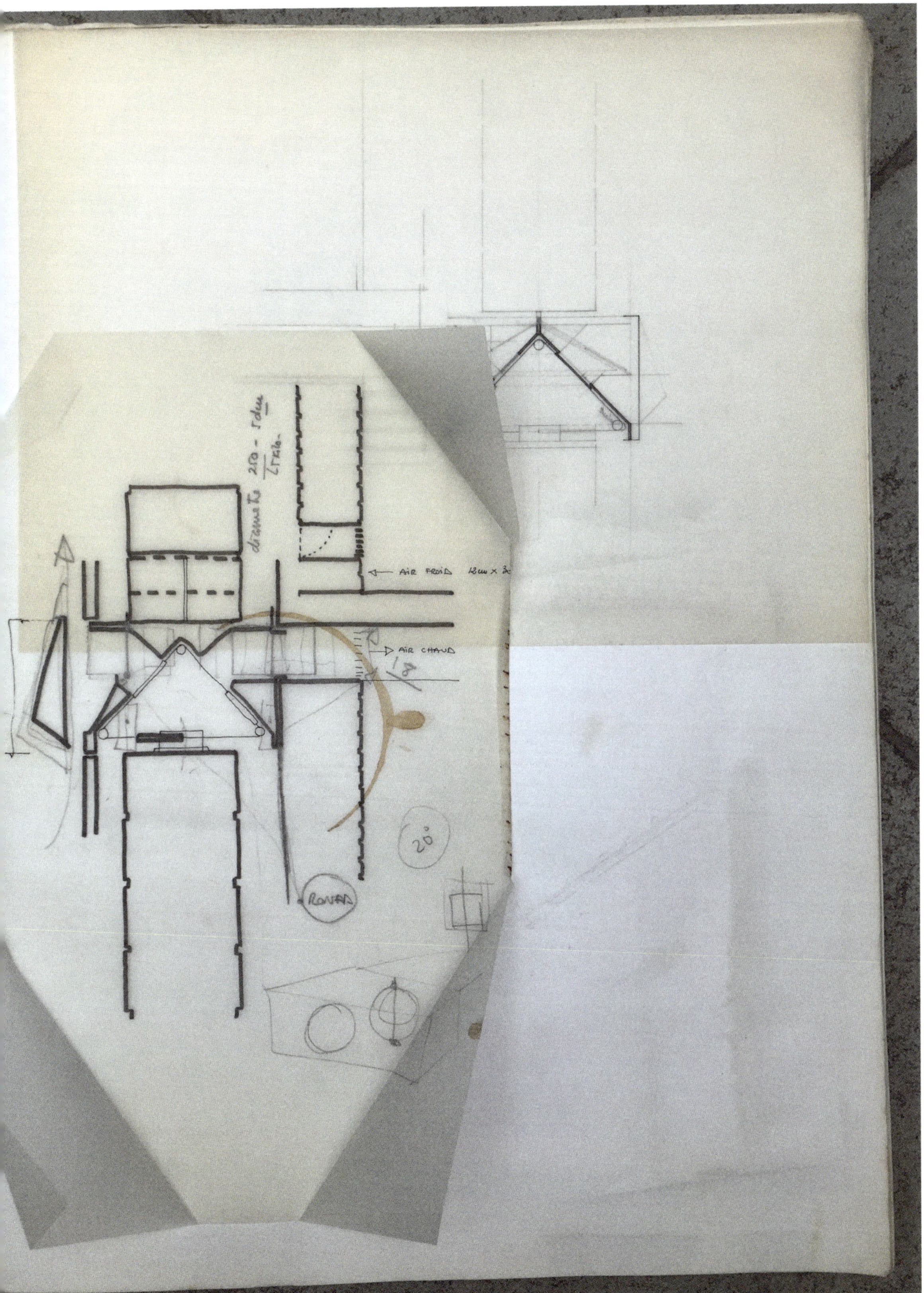
AIR FROID
AIR CHAUD
18
20°

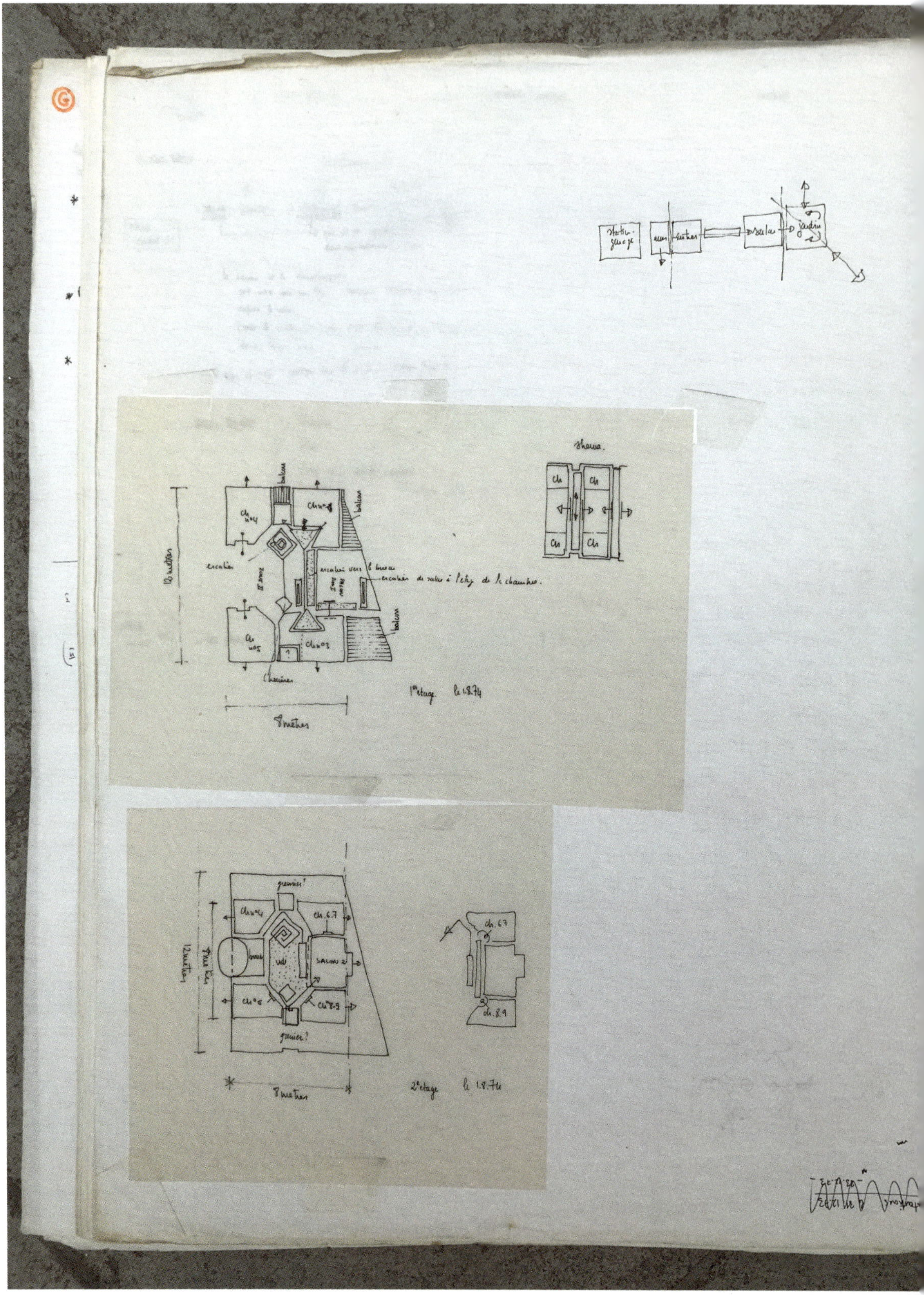
jardin
salon
escalier
balcon
Ch n°4
Ch n°5
Ch n°3
escalier vers le bureau
escalier de salon à l'étage de la chambre.
cheminée
8 mètres
1er étage. le 1.8.74
Ch
grenier?
Ch n°4
ch. 6.7
SALON 2
Ch n°5
Ch n°8-9
12 mètres
8 mètres
2e étage le 1.8.74
ch. 6.7
ch. 8.9

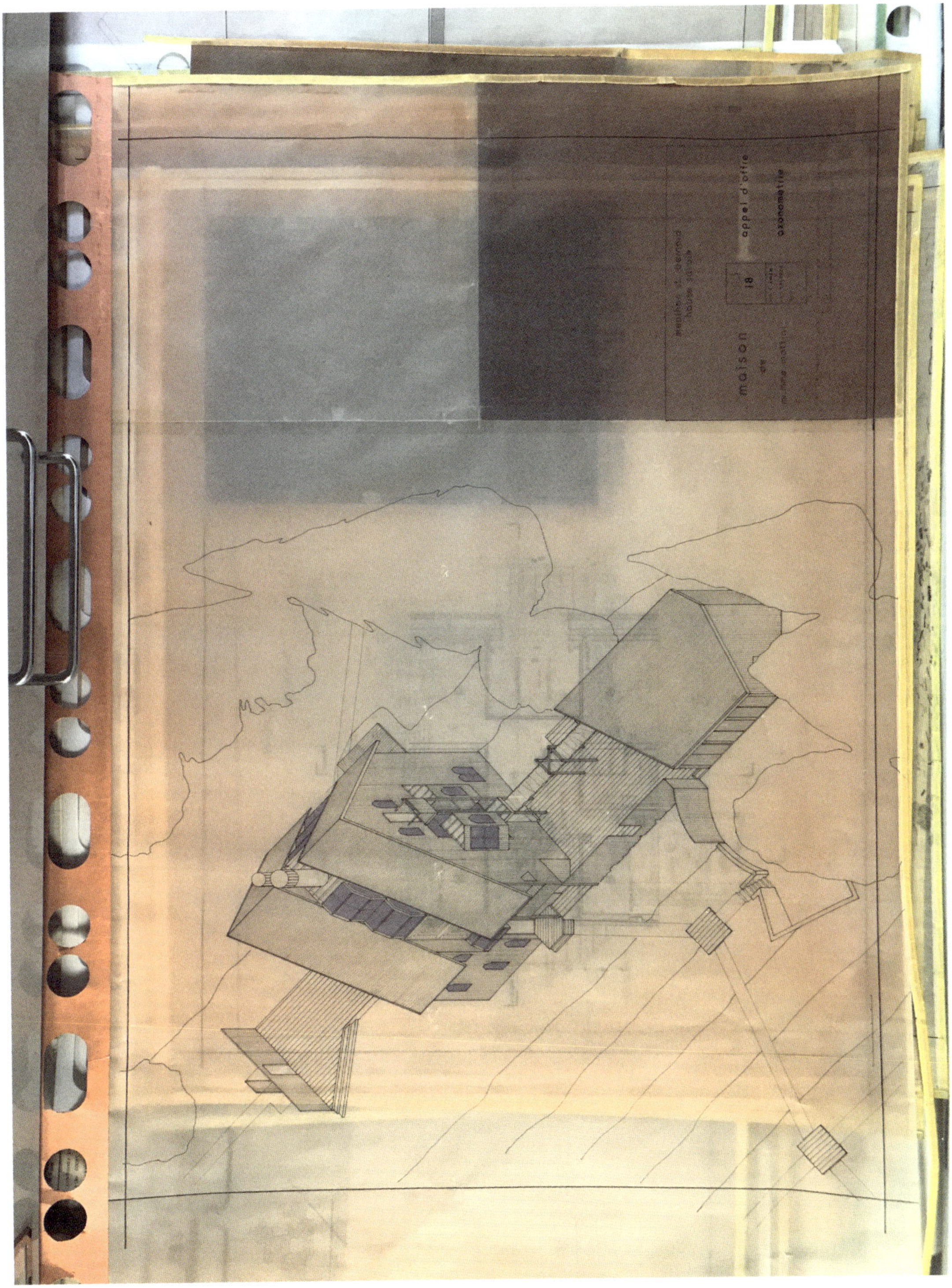
maison
de
18
appel d'offre
axonométrie

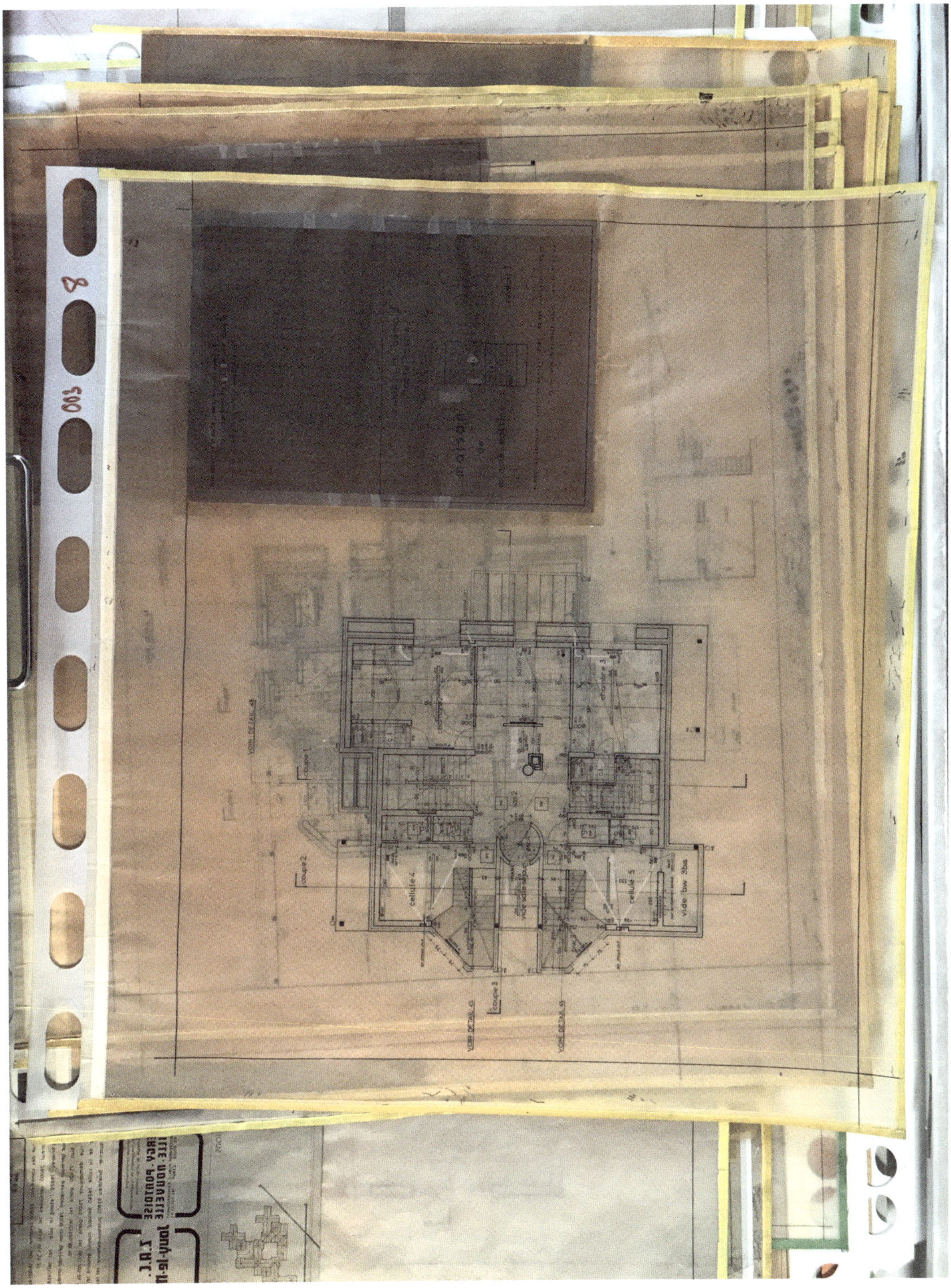

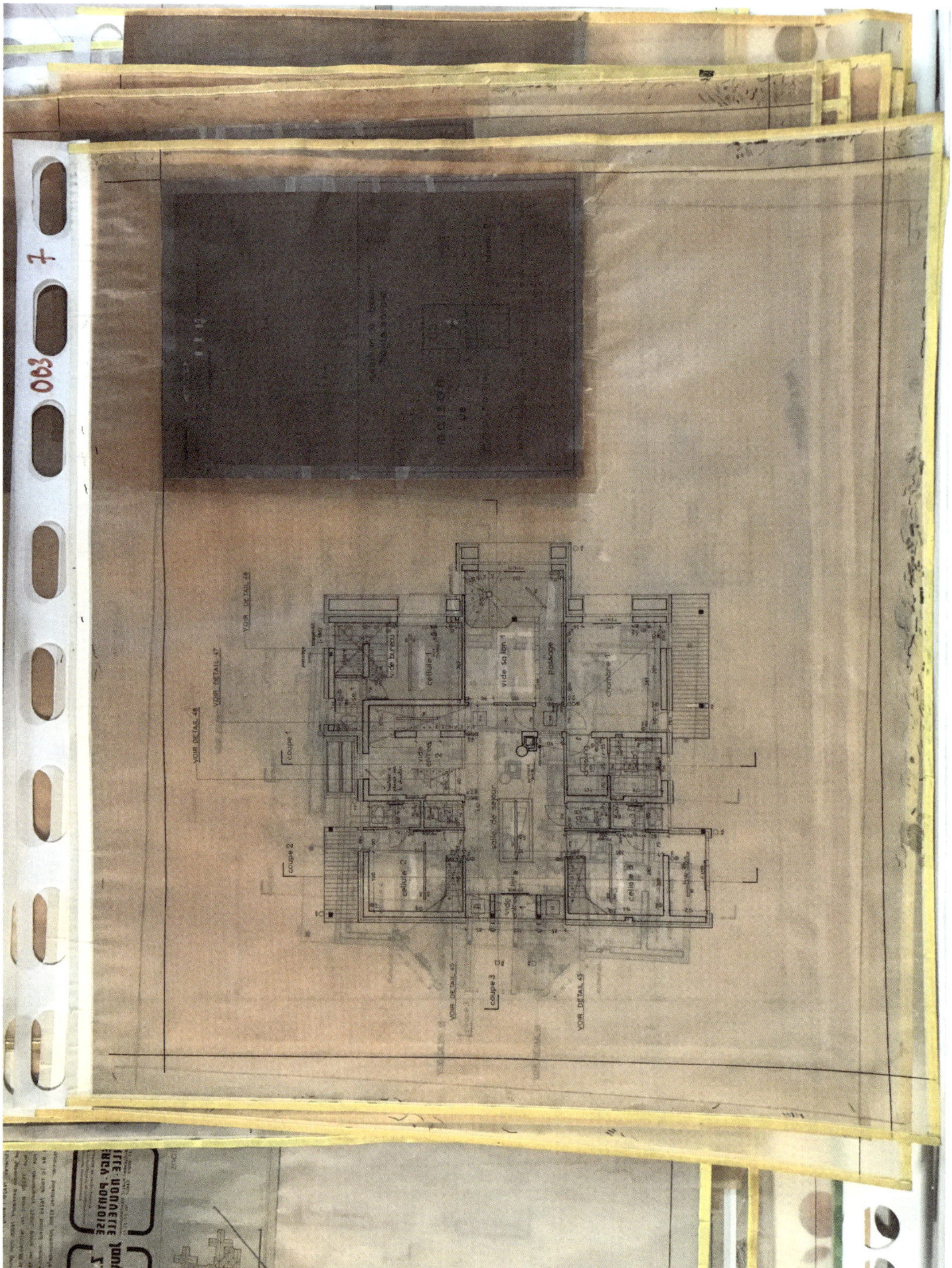

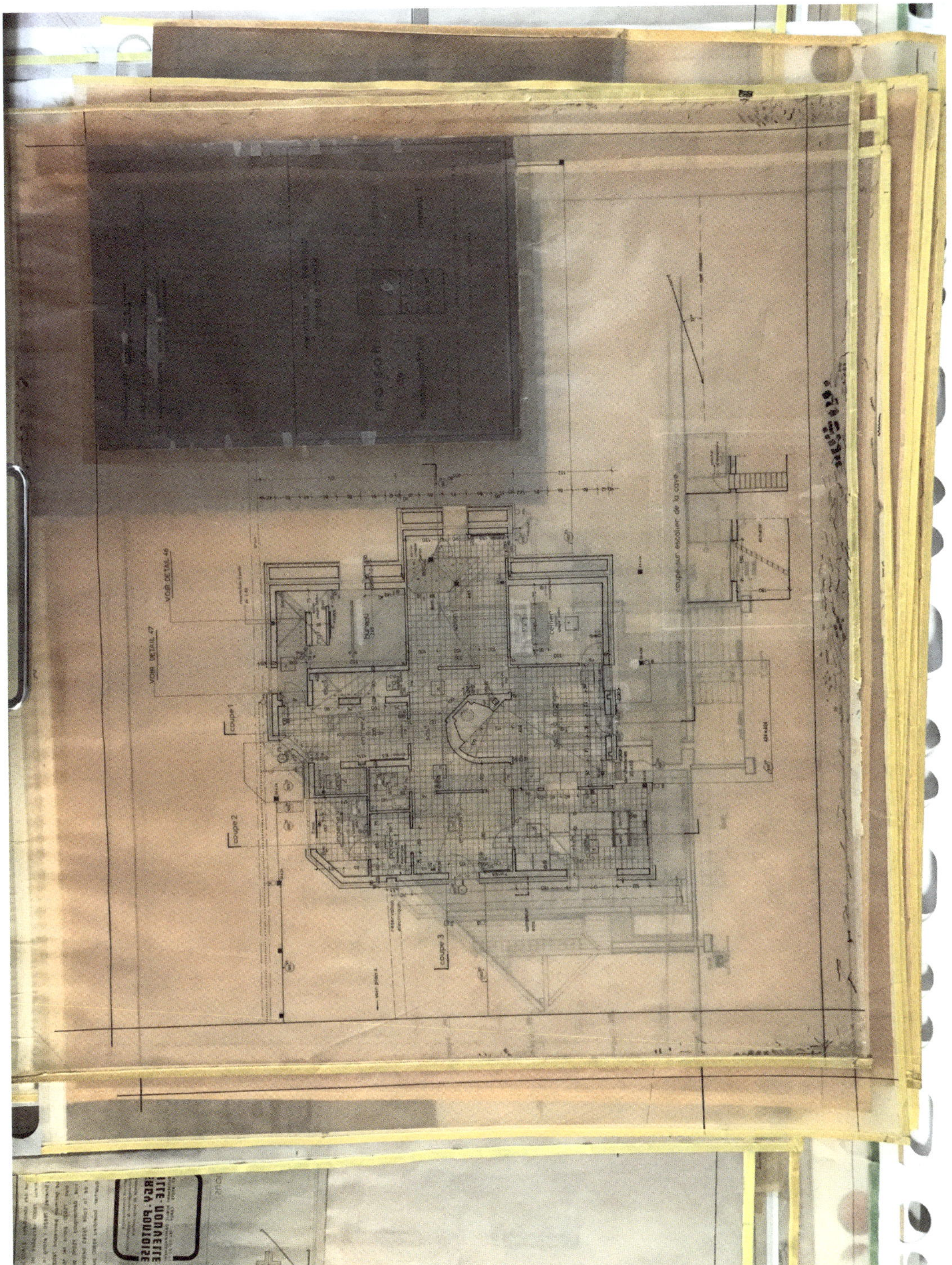

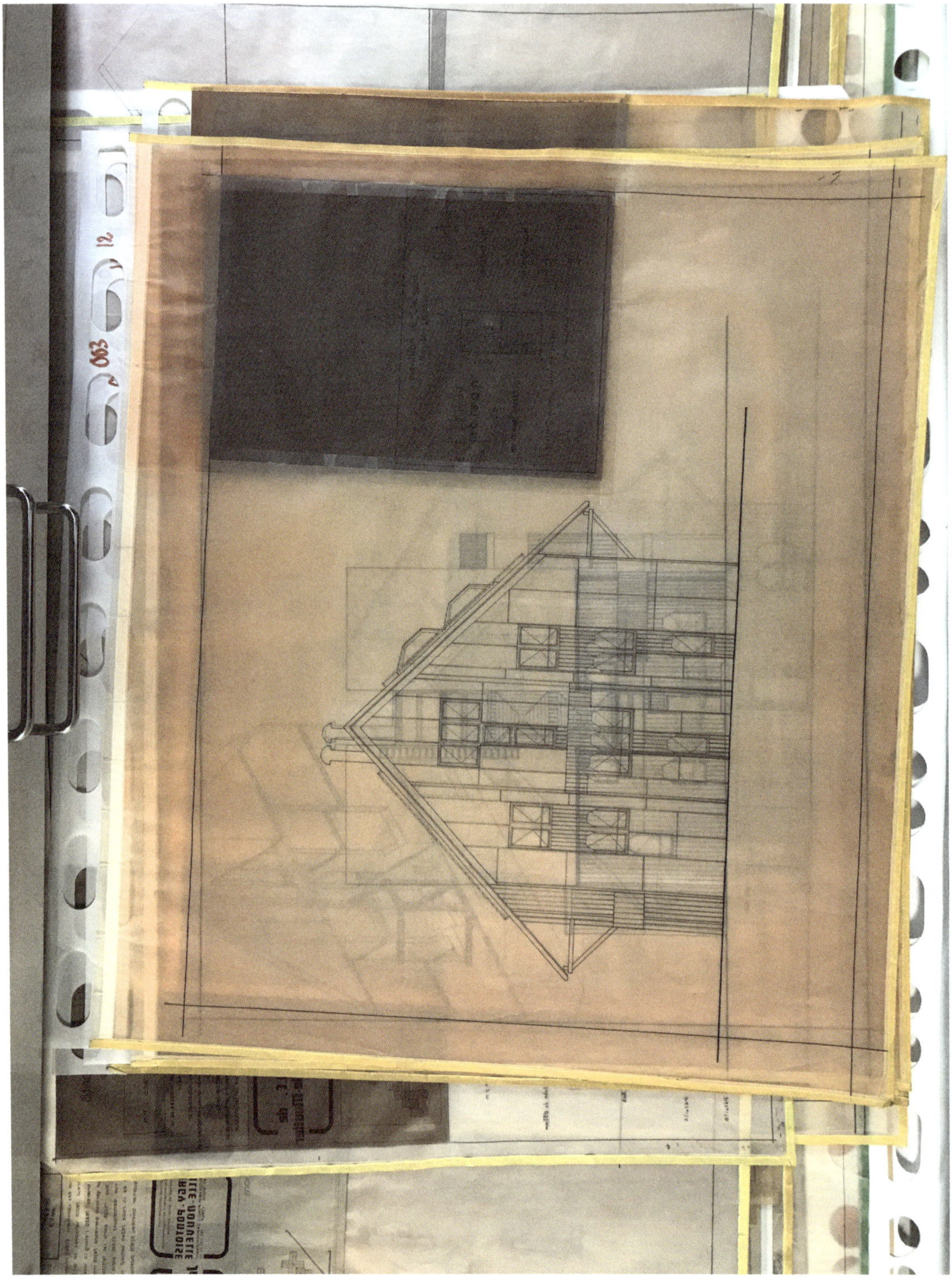

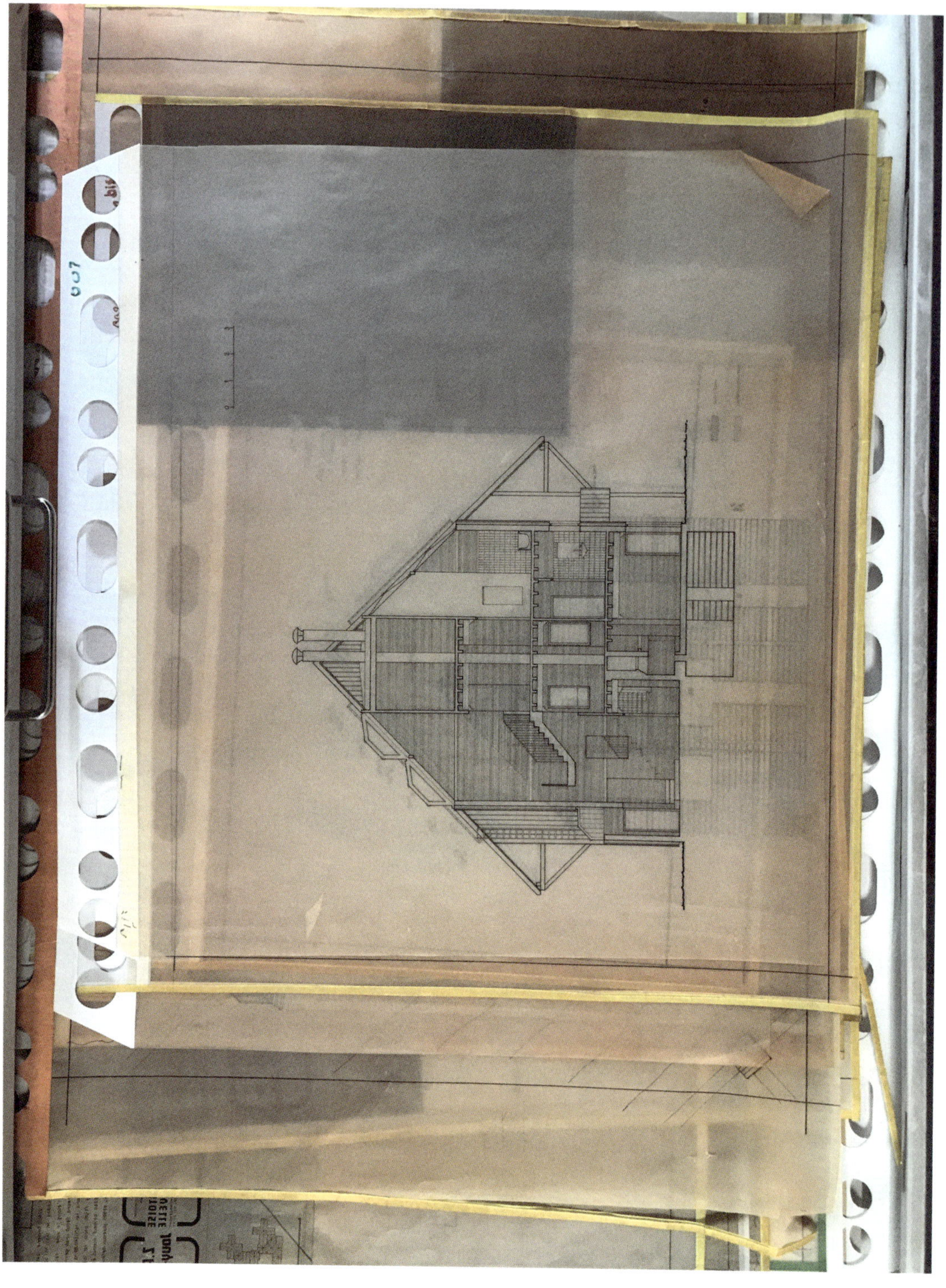

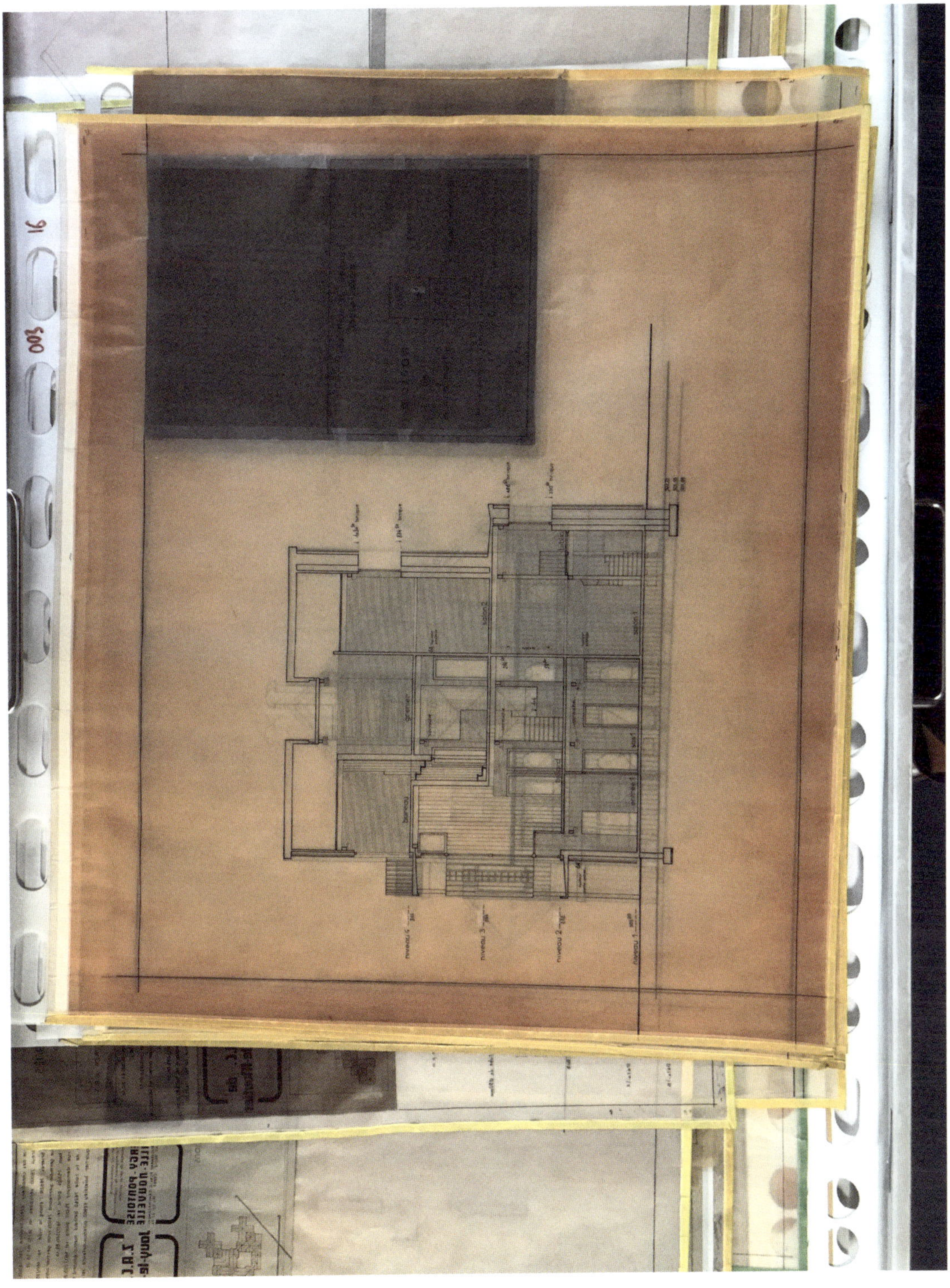

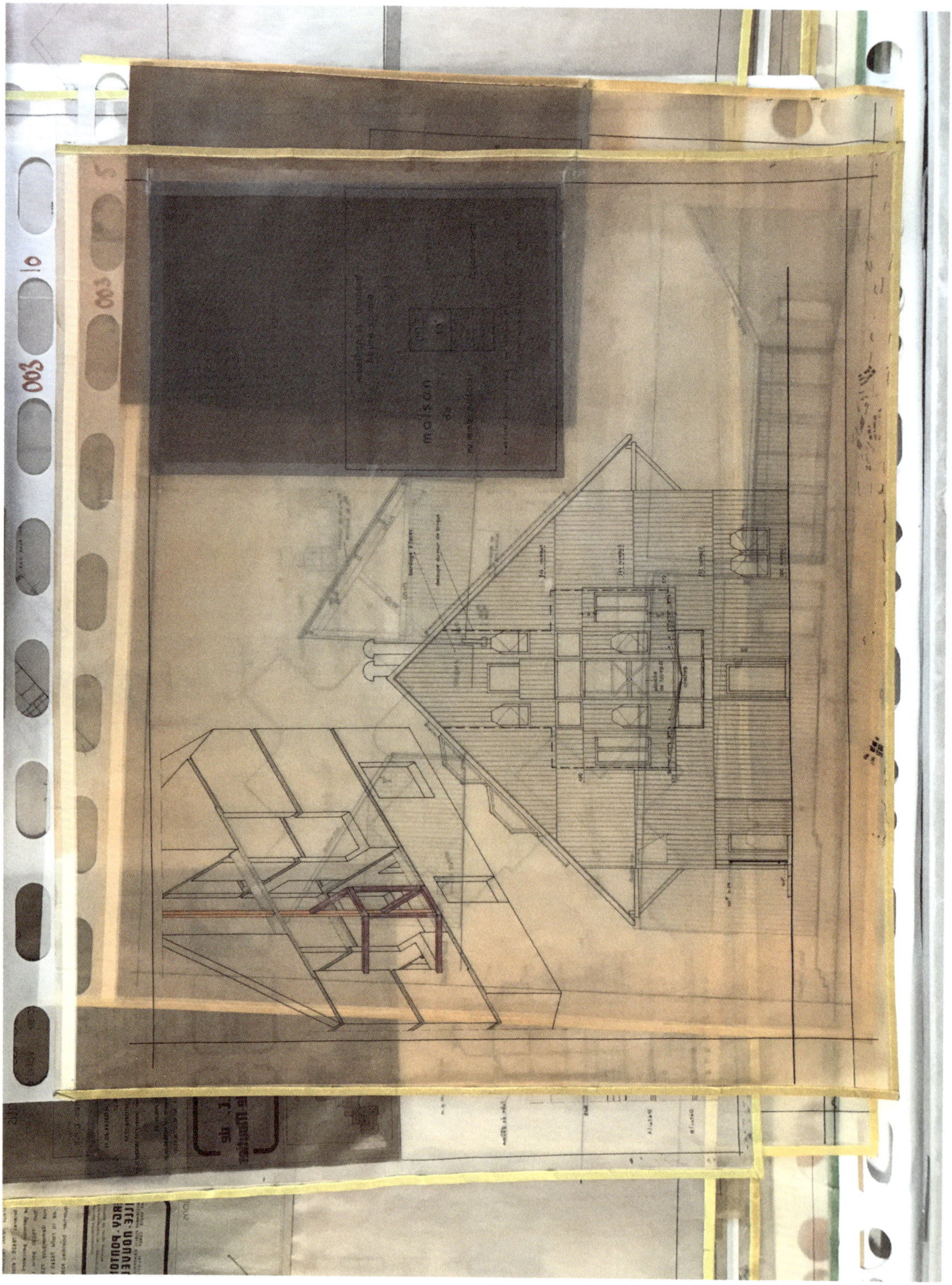

Maarten Delbeke

Matters of Ecology

Not without glee the short article on Mottini's *Maison Solaire* in *Architecture d'Aujourd'hui* cites the local authorities' objections to the project: "... taking into account its architectural conception and in particular of its volume, its height, the type of wood, the materials used and its baroque allure, this project would be, by its appearance, of such a nature as to undermine the character of the site ...". Together with reluctant building contractors, the technical challenge of devising a solar heating system, and the protracted design process—not to mention the circumstances of Mottini's own family life—the difficult process of obtaining a building permit added to a perhaps typical story of architectural strife in the face of adversity. Often such a story suggests that the project bears its scars, either triumphantly, when constrictions have been turned into assets, or with defiance, as signs of the sabotage short-sightedness has inflicted on intelligence and creativity.

In this case, however, the administrative objections provide an unexpected key for the interpretation of Mottini's project: it is accused of adopting a "baroque allure". The accusation is leveled without further specification, as if it is as easily understood as the remarks about dimensions and materials. Furthermore, in the same review we learn that Mottini was constrained to adopt the "standard volume, a kind of reduction of the form of traditional habitations [of the Haute-Savoie] for his house, sweetened with some signs of modern architecture, such as large bay windows". It smacks of irony that a building administration would dismiss the "baroque allure" of a building that forcibly interprets the traditional architecture of the Savoie, if anything a birthplace of baroque architecture. How then exactly did a holiday house for an extended family become "baroque"? What then does "baroque allure" mean? Excessive posturing and unwarranted ornamentation? At the risk of giving too much weight to what might amount to a quick put-down penned by an ill-disposed official, it is worth exploring what 'baroqueness' could signify in this particular context.

In 1967 the critic and historian Pierre Charpentrat published a small book, *Le mirage baroque*, an examination of how and why the notion 'baroque' had become commonplace in French culture after

World War II. Charpentrat registered the presence of the word in debates about topics as diverse as modern jazz and Catholic liturgy, noting how it could become associated with ideas ranging from the hyper-conservative to the progressive. On the most fundamental level, Charpentrat asserted that the embrace of 'baroque' pointed towards a particular turn in the French psyche; a recognition—for better or worse—of the existence of an 'otherness' which is part of, and yet in tension with an equally mythical and supposedly innate French 'classicism'. What Charpentrat described and criticized, is the French desire to engage with this otherness in the wake of the historical rupture of the Second World War, while maintaining a slightly superior distance by casting this otherness as 'baroque'.

Besides this cultural criticism, Charpentrat explored the baroque from a related yet different perspective: as a critic and a historian of architecture. Having authored three monographs on the 'historical' baroque—European architecture of the 17th and 18th centuries—Charpentrat also wrote extensively on contemporary architecture, where he drew a clear parallel between baroque and modernism. In his view, both periods are characterized by a break with history. Perhaps more importantly, Charpentrat also recognized a similarity in the baroque and modernist dealings with space; not as understood by Sigfried Giedion, who discovered in the architecture of Francesco Borromini premonitions of modernist spatial experiments, but as forms of functionalism. In Charpentrat's view, the baroque was the architectural answer to the new prerequisites of function and representation that characterized the 17th and 18th century, just like modernism took on the demands of a changing society. Baroque and modernist functionalism, so Charpentrat argued, share a fundamentally anti-academic attitude towards this challenge, which affords them an architectural freedom their classicist counterparts lack.

Regardless of whether the official who condemned Mottini's project was aware of the meanings and associations that had accrued around the word 'baroque', he denounced the "baroque allure" of *Maison Solaire* in the cultural context analyzed by Charpentrat. If the epithet 'baroque' allowed him to disavow the formal characteristics of the project, he also conveyed a sense of strangeness, of not belonging. Despite adopting the general shape of a rural house in Savoy, the building seems somehow out of place. Why would that be the case?

The plan of Solaris is almost an exercise in decomposition. It doesn't open up the interior towards a view, nor does it concentrate the bedrooms and wet cells in a single zone of the house, but proposes a division of the main surface into nine quadrangles of similar size. These are further divided into smaller strips that allow for the integration of vertical circulation and services. There is an intricate development of the third dimension, especially in the design of the main staircase and the interior first-floor balcony with its adjacent small gallery.

But the house is first and foremost a stack of living cells each with their own amenities, a logic that is most visible in the ground floor, where the parceling of the surface divides the different components of the programme into discrete units. With the two entrances on the north and the east, the ground floor is a conglomeration of rooms each of a quite different nature, from dining room to an almost autonomous duplex apartment, arranged around a central space defined by the volume of the fireplace. This space appears less as the actual and symbolic center of the house than as a distribution point connecting the otherwise separate components.

The conglomeration of cells is anchored to the south wall. Acting as the collector of solar energy, the south façade consists of polychrome glazing mounted on an aluminum frame. This glazing is essential to the functioning of the collector, but also gives a particular architectural expression to the house. While it signals the modernity of the Maison Solaire, it does not present itself as a piece of technology but rather as the emblem of the house. As such, it creates an intricate relationship with the other facades and the exterior as a whole. In seeming contrast with the wooden cladding of the remaining faces of the Maison, it also draws attention to how these 'traditional' facades depart from historical precedent and signal their own modernity, for instance in the way the wooden cladding frames the windows. The two types of openings, the idiosyncratic arched windows and larger window panes, also confound the perception of the scale of the building, again challenging expectations and reading habits. The roof, in turn, is divided into two sections by means of a glass section. Similar to the facades, it communicates that the house is not a charade of a traditional farm nor a building determined by modern technology, but a particular entity almost forcibly pressed into this volume. Roof and facades are less compositions shaped by the rhythm of a construction system or the habits of the vernacular, than surfaces punched through by the different cells of the interior and their extensions.

Mottini's preliminary studies for the house confirm that Solaris is the result of a painstaking process of decomposition and conglomeration. Over the course of many years and numerous revisions, Mottini analyzed in minute detail not only the future site of the house or the construction of its heating system, but also the complex relationships that characterized the family that would inhabit it. Mottini's medium is as much the written word as the diagram, the photograph or the drawing, especially when it comes to the painstaking description of the domestic spheres that would suit the various family members. The texts read as a form of psychological analysis which is immediately mined for its spatial consequences; a structuralist approach that is equally evident in the careful reading of the site to determine the optimal approach to the house, the research into the structure and the heating system, and finally in the studies for the facades, which appear as compositions of related surfaces rather than representations of material objects.

The consequences of Mottini's reading of the family are most evident in the pair of living units on the south side. The unit to the east was destined for the father, and occupies two floors with their own internal staircase. It is literally a house (or a hut) within the house, a place for withdrawal and even isolation. The western unit is reached by means of a free-standing staircase that gives onto the small gallery overlooking the central spaces of the ground floor; conceived as the abode for the mother, it has its own adjacent bathroom. Strikingly, the gallery is closed off from the central first landing with a door, affording a form of separation from the family life unfolding there. This play with spatial and visual connections and separations is rooted directly in Mottini's understanding of the family dynamics, in this instance specifically, the position of the two parents. Over the course of the design process, changing dynamics required revisions of the project, until they finally coalesced in its present form.

House Solaris is shaped by the overlapping interests and desires that drove its designer. It is a building of intentions and orchestrated incidents. In one striking moment, the internal staircases of the two first floor duplexes on the north protrude from the façade in order to achieve the internal connection. This incident illustrates a more general characteristic of the project: the dynamic relationship between interiority and exteriority. This is not a single unit, a house or a home, but a reminiscence of such an entity that consists of multiple layers which turn towards and away from each other. Mottini has organized this constellation according to its orientation towards the sun, the characteristics of the site, and the social structure of its inhabitants. As such, *Maison Solaire* is a study of two ecologies: of the post-War French family, and of the Savoie habitat and its resources, both natural and historical. Expressed in the terms of Charpentrat's baroque, the house evinces the irruption of modernity into well-established traditions, both architecturally and socially. Like the Maison Solaire, the Savoy farm housed multiple generations, but Mottini's project fully accounts for the complicated and diverse dynamics of a family life determined by modern expectations with regard to communality, privacy and occupancy. At the same time, the *Maison Solaire* displays the presence and importance of energy management, not just as a discrete system but as a formal device. Finally, the irruption of modernity into tradition is not just accepted and 'solved', but given architectural form. There is a sustained intentionality in the design that celebrates the complexity of its own assignment. Nowhere is the project allowed to run on its own; the potential irruption of the designer's intentions is always there. In a truly baroque paradox, the designer declares his presence because of his almost obsessive attention to the conditions of his brief. It is this paradox that gives *Maison Solaire* its baroque allure.

References:

"Maison à Menthon Saint-Bernard, Lac d'Annecy." *Architecture d'Aujourd'hui* 209 (June 1980), theme: *Solaire passif ou actif*, 24–26.

Pierre Charpentrat, *Le mirage baroque.* Paris: Minuit, 1967.

On the French interpretation of 'baroque', with an excellent reading of Charpentrat's work: Philippe Minguet, *France Baroque.* Paris: Hazan, 1988.

On Charpentrat's understanding of 'functionalism', see Jean-Pierre Martinon, "Pierre Charpentrat et la question du fonctionnalisme baroque." *Baroque. Revue internationale. Journées internationales d'étude du baroque* 9–10 (1980): 112–115.